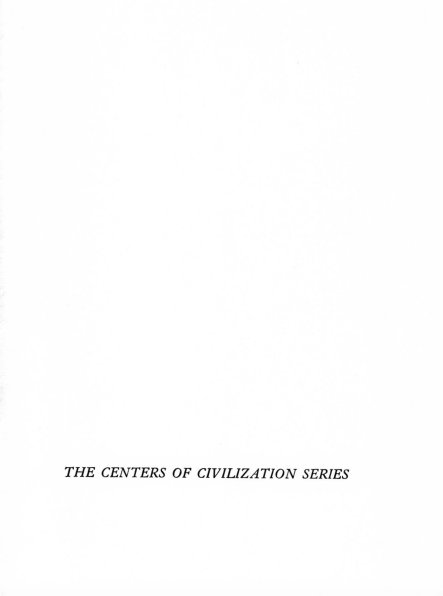

THE CENTERS OF CIVILIZATION SERIES

Baghdad

METROPOLIS OF THE ABBASID CALIPHATE

Baghdad

METROPOLIS OF THE ABBASID CALIPHATE

by
GASTON WIET

Translated by Seymour Feiler

UNIVERSITY OF OKLAHOMA PRESS : NORMAN

The author, the translator, and the publisher owe a special debt of gratitude to Mr. Richard Ettinghausen of the Department of Islamic Art, The Metropolitan Museum of Art, New York City, for reading the galley proofs and making important corrections and suggestions.

INTERNATIONAL STANDARD BOOK NUMBER: 0–8061–0922–x

LIBRARY OF CONGRESS CATALOG CARD NUMBER: 72–123348

CONTENTS

Baghdad

METROPOLIS OF THE ABBASID CALIPHATE

1.

THE FIRST CAPITALS OF ISLAM

"From the time they first appeared on the historical scene," wrote William Marçais, "the Moslems proved to be builders of cities. There is hardly another civilization in which one finds so much urban construction with names and dates characterizing the undertaking as a planned activity. One has only to mention Kufa, Basra, Wasit, Mosul, Baghdad, Fostat, Cairo, and Shiraz in the east, and, in the Maghreb, Qairawan, Mahdia, Algiers, Oran, Yiaret, Tlemcen, Fez, Marrakesh, Qal'a, Bougie, and Rabat. We should note in passing that, of the twenty cities that I have just enumerated, fifteen are still in existence today. That adds up to quite a success."

The effort was expended, for the most part, to establish general or regional political capitals. Mohammed set the example by abandoning Mecca, his native city, and settling in Medina. Actually, the latter was already in existence; the originality consisted of giving it a new name, Madinat al-Nabi, the City of the Prophet, from which we get Medina.

Mohammed's first three successors maintained the pre-eminence of the city, but Ali, who succeeded to the throne in 656, no longer feeling safe in Arabia, emigrated to the Lower Mesopotamian city of Kufa, which had been founded by the Arabs less than twenty years before. Louis Massignon wrote, "Kufa was to become in the early days of Islam the most active center of that social phenomenon, the sedentarization of the Bedouins, and the capital of the development of Moslem civilization."

The Arab miracle had begun, and the armies of the caliphs of Medina rushed off in two directions simultaneously, toward Iran and toward Syria and Egypt. The spectacular successes could have been seriously compromised by the civil war which was to bleed Islam in its early days. Mu'awiya, the son of Abu Sufyan, long the implacable enemy of the Apostle of God in Mecca, was ready to revolt against Ali's authority. When his rival was assassinated, Mu'awiya proclaimed himself caliph and succeeded in founding a dynasty called Umayyad, after the name of one of his ancestors. Anxious to avoid clan fights and local quarrels, Mu'awiya chose Damascus as his residence. Ruling over encamped armed tribesmen who owned no land, he did his best to prevent tribal outbreaks, the cause of great hatred. As sovereign, he administered recently conquered regions whose populations were neither Arab nor quite yet Moslem, and like the first generals of the heroic period, he sanctioned the customs of local government and kept the old officials.

The family of caliphs played an essential role in every domain. The onward rush of the Arab armies never let up; constantly renewed waves of assailants surged forward after each halt. Evidence of this is seen when in 750, at the time of the collapse of the Umayyad caliphate, the Arab armies reached the Atlantic and conquered the Iberian Peninsula, while in the east they occupied all the territory extending up to central Asia.

This rule, which can still be called Arab, was carried to its greatest splendor by men of the highest order. They were capable of riding out storms, only the worst of which will be mentioned here as an example of how their minds worked. They struggled against the Alid legitimists and the Kharijite revolutionaries and, incidentally, against a third party composed of malcontents whose chief wanted to move the caliphate back to Arabia.

The flexibility of the Umayyad statesmen permitted them to grant a certain amount of liberty to their subjects while clothing themselves in the ancient garments of Islam. Thus, under a lenient administration, the non-Moslems were governed according to the norms of the past, and official documents continued to be published in the different national languages.

The rate of the subject peoples' conversion to the new religion, however, was fairly rapid. The number of Moslems was still quite small at the end of the seventh century, and it varied from region to region, but conversions continued at a steady pace. Through their ultimate political goal of Arabization by administrative means, the Umayyads finally gained an audience ready to listen to Koranic preaching.

These caliphs, too, must be given credit for having made the first contact with Iranian thought and with the scientific works of antiquity. These first profitable approaches led to the great period of translations, an era that can be considered the golden age of Abbasid rule. It was to Persia and especially to Mesopotamia, stirred up by heresiarchs and pietist missionaries, that the Umayyads sent their best governors, who were equally severe and competent. Recruited for these confidential posts were talented men, who were not afraid of being unpopular.

The task of the governors was a delicate one. Society had indeed become complex. The conquering Arabs, constituting the actual nation, had very decided feelings of superiority over the natives, who retained their way of life without being molested and who were cared for, since it was they who paid most of the taxes.

These "protégés," who became Moslems en masse in the first half of the eighth century, were to break out of the ranks and form an anti-Arab movement. Since the members of the opposition could not agree among themselves, the central power was to win out, but not before a great deal of propaganda had converged to attack its authority.

Iran had suffered a frightful invasion, but the country was not resigned to defeat. Among the people of Khurasan, which had been selected by government policy as a place of exile for the most active Alids, it was very easy to gather recruits for the fight against central authority. Some of them were motivated by a spirit of revenge against the Arab conquest. The Shi'ites, tenacious partisans of legitimacy who favored the descendants of the ill-starred Ali, thought they were supporting the cause of the Alid family. Opposition to the Syrians was for the Persians a continuation of traditional anti-Byzantine hostility.

The rebellion was openly proclaimed in 747 after a period of underground propaganda. It was probably not by mere chance that the instigator, Abu Muslim, established his headquarters at Merv in Khurasan, the very city where the unfortunate Yezdegerd, the last Sassanian king, had died.

A hectic, even dangerous existence no doubt answered the best hopes of the Persian people. The success of the plots indicates that the admirably conducted conspiracy against the Arab caliphate was an old one. The harangues of the various agitators reached an element of the population that asked for nothing more than to join up and carry banners. One can very well speak of Abu Muslim's blackshirts, for the Abbasid partisans adopted a uniform of that color. The faithful flocked in from all sides. Their clothes and even some of the clubs with which they were armed were dyed black. Theophanes calls them the Khurasanian Maurophores. Louis Massignon shows that this army, recruited in eastern Persia, was trained like the Theban legion "in misogynous discipline."

We know the end of the story: the Umayyad dynasty collapsed after a battle which took place on the banks of the Great Zab, not far from the Arbela battlefield. It is of little importance that Marwan II, the last Umayyad caliph, escaped to Egypt.

2

THE FOUNDING OF BAGHDAD

THE DYNASTY THAT TOOK OVER from the Umayyads was called Abbasid—a reminder that it was descended from Abbas, a paternal uncle of the Prophet. The first caliph, Saffah, went to Iraq to settle, and he chose as his capital Kufa, already a famous city founded in the early days of Islam. There was probably friction between the Khurasanian guard and the local inhabitants, who had been ungovernable in the days of the caliph Ali. This friction could also have been the reason for three other successive and rapid moves of the caliphate which terminated in the founding of Baghdad. It is not by mere chance that the city has a Persian name. It was originally a retrenched camp where the caliph lived in safety under the protection of his Khurasanians.

The description left by Ya'qubi one and one-half centuries after the city's founding deserves to be reported in its entirety. Undoubtedly it is a piece of bravura, but it contains evident truths that are of some use.

"I mention Baghdad first of all because it is the heart of Iraq, and, with no equal on earth either in the Orient or the Occident, it is the most extensive city in area, in importance, in prosperity, in abundance of water, and in healthful climate. It is inhabited by the most diverse individuals, both

8

city people and country folk; people emigrate to it from all countries, both near and far; and everywhere there are men who have preferred it to their own country. All the peoples of the world have their own neighborhoods there, their trade and commercial centers; that is why there is gathered together here what does not exist in any other city in the world. It stretches out on the two banks of those two large rivers, the Tigris and the Euphrates, and watches commercial products and staples flow to it on land and on water. For it is with great ease that each commercial object is transported endlessly from East and West, from Moslem and non-Moslem regions. Indeed, merchandise is brought from India, Sind, China, Tibet, the land of the Turks, the Khazars, and the Abyssinians—from everywhere in short—to such a degree that it is found in greater profusion in Baghdad than in its country of origin. It is procured so easily and surely that one would think that all the goods of the earth are sent there, all the treasures of the world gathered there, and all the blessings of the universes concentrated there.

"Besides, it is the capital of the Abbasids, the center of their empire, and the seat of their sovereignty, where no one has appeared before them, and where no other princes have lived.

"Its name is famous and its reputation is universally known. Iraq is indeed the center of the world. For, according to the unanimous opinion of the astronomers exposed in the writing of the ancient sages, it is located in the fourth climate, the median climate, where the temperature equals itself by epochs and by seasons. It is extremely hot during summer days, the cold is intense during winter days, and a moderate temperature is enjoyed in autumn and in spring; the change from autumn to winter and from spring to summer takes place without violent contrasts. Thus the passing of the seasons brings repeated and regular variations of temperature. Not only is the climate regular but the terrain is excellent, the water is sweet, the trees flourish, the fruit is of perfect quality, the harvests are magnificent, good things abound, and the water supply is almost at ground level. As a result of this normal temperature, of the quality of the soil, of the freshness of the water, the inhabitants are of a happy disposition, their countenances are bright, and their intelligence is of an open nature. The people also excel through their knowledge, their understanding, their good education, their perspicacity, their distinction, their commercial, industrial, and business sense, their ingenuousness in all controversy, their competence in all trades, and their ability in all industry. No one is better educated than their scholars, better informed than their authorities in tradition, more solid in their syntax than their grammarians, more supple than their singers, more certain than their readers of the Koran, more expert than their physicians, more capable than their calligraphers, clearer than their logicians, more zealous than their ascetics, better jurists than their magistrates, more eloquent than their preachers, more artistic than their poets, or more voluptuous than their gay blades."

This is doubtless exaggerated appreciation, and some of the points should be taken with reservations. Legend even has the founder of the city, the caliph Mansur, make this wonderful prediction:

"This is indeed the city that I am to found, where I am to live, and where my descendants will reign afterward. Princes had lost all track of it, before and since Islam, so that the previsions and orders of God could be accomplished through my efforts; thus traditions are confirmed, signs and prognostics become clear. Assuredly, this *island*, bounded on the east by the Tigris and on the west by the Euphrates, will prove to be the crossroads of the universe. Ships on the Tigris, coming from Wasit, Obolla, Ahwaz, Fars, Oman, Yamama, Bahrein, and neighboring countries will land and drop anchor there. It is there that merchandise will arrive by way of the Tigris from Mosul, Azerbaijan, and Armenia; that too will be the destination of products transported by ship on the Euphrates from Raqqa, Syria, the borderlands of Asia Minor, Egypt, and the Maghreb. This city will also be on the route of the peoples of Jebel, Ispahan, and of the provinces of Khurasan. I shall erect this capital and live in it all my life. It will be the residence of my descendants; it will certainly be the most prosperous city in the world."

It is appropriate to compare this enthusiasm with the judgment of a contemporary orientalist who is no less laudatory. Jean Sauvaget writes: "The founding of Baghdad, and then of Samarra, completely transformed marketing conditions; conveniently well placed to maintain relations by sea with southern Asia, these large cities, exceptionally well populated for the time, sheltered the Abbasid court containing all the members of the caliph's family and gathered together in one spot thousands of people used to living in mad splendor."

These excerpts have the great advantage of showing that the site of the new city contained all the necessary conditions for the security and the development of a political and economic capital, since its location gave it control over strategic and commercial routes. Situated between two rivers, Baghdad believed that it was protected from invasion and thought that its name, Madinat-al-Salam, the City of Peace (or City of Safety), was justified. This was indeed the official name of the Abbasid capital as it appeared on coins as well as on the cloth manufactured in the weaving shops of the caliphate. The name was a deliberate reminder of an expression in the Koran (VI, 127), *Dar-el-Salam*, which refers to Paradise.

The observation was made to Caliph Mansur himself: "Commander of the Faithful, you will live between two rivers so that your enemies will be able to reach you only by crossing a wooden or stone bridge; when the wooden bridge is cut or the stone bridge is demolished, your enemy will not be able to approach you."

Later events will show that such reasoning was a little naïve. The important fact is that the two rivers were to facilitate the transportation of men and goods. It should not be forgotten that Basra, a port for ships going to China and India, was near by.

Mas'udi's speech is no less lyrical: "It is the most excellent region on earth as far as essential needs and food are concerned. For the most precious possessions in the world, after safety, honor, and power, are pure water and air. Besides, the best rivers in the world are the Tigris and the Euphrates, and the best spot on earth has always been the confluence of the Tigris and the Euphrates."

The plans for the new capital had been drawn up under the direction of Khalid ibn Barmak, the head of a family that distinguished itself, then ended miserably, under the reign of Harun al-Rashid. Ya'qubi's account of the founding of Baghdad on a site which was not far from the old Sassanian capital has the terseness of a police report:

"The caliph Mansur assembled engineers, men with a reputation in the art of construction, and surveyors skillful in measuring lengths and surfaces and in dividing up land in order to draw up the plans of the capital which was called the City of Abu Ja'far (Mansur). When all the workers that he had called arrived, the masons, the woodworkers, the carpenters, the blacksmiths, the laborers, he distributed payment in kind and determined salaries. He had written requests sent out everywhere asking that everyone be sent to him who knew the construction trade even slightly; one hundred thousand different workers and artisans came to him. The plans were laid out in the month of July of the year 758. It was a round city, the only circular city known in the entire world. The foundations were laid at the moment chosen by the astronomers Naubakht and Mashallah. Arab writers are proud of it, and the following remarks are attributed to Jahiz: 'I have visited the greatest cities and those that are the most remarkable in architecture and solidity in the provinces of Syria, in the countries of the Greeks and still others, but I have never seen a city raised to greater heights and more perfectly round, with wider gates, or with such imposing walls.' "

Most authors speak of the founding date as having been four years later (762). Massignon chose July 23, 762, under the sign of the Lion and the horoscope of Sagittarius, for the beginning of the work that created Baghdad, the "Gift of God," which did not take, or retake, a Persian name by mere chance. Even with the large numbers of workers, construction went on for some time. The year 765 seems to have been the date when the caliph actually took up residence in Baghdad.

The city was to be built of brick, the basic material of the country. Even before the foundations were laid, large, square bricks were manufactured measuring about eighteen inches on each side, while the half-brick was oblong and about nine inches wide. Abu Hanifa, a founder of one of the four Moslem schools of jurisprudence, was appointed to count the bricks, and he contrived a measuring device to help. A carefully constructed canal brought water to the work site for both human consumption and the manufacture of bricks.

The caliph himself named the city's four gates for the destinations to which they gave access: Kufa (the starting point for pilgrimages), Basra, Khurasan, and Syria. The distance between diametrically opposite gates was a little less than one and one-fourth miles. The gates had double iron doors that were so heavy they required several men to open and close them. Open, the gates were high enough to allow a horseman carrying a banner or a lance to pass through.

The wall between the gates, made of brick with clay used as mortar, was about 145 feet thick at its base and about 39 feet thick at its top. This wall was about 98 feet high, including the merlons. It was surrounded by an impressive thick outer wall, at a distance of about 165 feet, which was flanked at intervals by solid towers and was surmounted by rounded merlons. The outer wall was protected by a strong, solid glacis made of baked bricks and quicklime. Beyond that was a water-filled moat. The outer wall was demolished at the end of the ninth century by order of the caliph Mu'tadid, and although its destruction was stopped for a while because of certain protests, riverside inhabitants gradually began to settle on the site. It seems, therefore, that the original plan of the city disappeared at that time.

Wide avenues, bordered by brick and plaster arcades, ran in four directions from the center of the city to the city's entrances. One could enter each through a vaulted passageway, built of baked bricks and plaster, in the outer wall. A roadway of hard stone led from there to a passageway through the main wall which was closed by iron gates. The passageway had small windows which let light in but kept rain out.

Each of the four gates was vaulted, and each of the entranceways of the main wall was surmounted by an immense gilt cupola, an observation tower on teak columns. Each tower had rooms which were reached by a ramp.

In the middle of the city's central square was the Golden Gate Palace. Over the central part of this building was a green dome about 160 feet high, on top of which was a horseman holding a lamp. It was commonly believed that the statue had magical powers. Its presence is mysterious, for it is not mentioned after about 758 until it fell during a violent storm in 941. After the death of the caliph Amin in 813, the palace no longer served as the caliph's residence, and it fell into ruins in 1255.

At first the palace was surrounded by a vast esplanade onto which only the caliph could come on horseback; near by were a few private mansions and officers' residences. On the side toward the Gate of Syria was a building reserved for the guards and a long, large portico, made of baked bricks and marble, which rested on columns. The palace governor lived in the latter and the commander of the guards in the former.

The cathedral mosque adjoined the palace. It was built of sun-baked bricks and clay; its roof rested on wooden columns. The building was rebuilt by order of the caliph Harun al-Rashid in 893. This was the building seen by Ibn Rusteh and described as having been "built of fire-baked bricks and plaster, with a teakwood roof painted the color of lapis lazuli, supported by pillars of the same wood." Repairs later made by the caliph Mu'tadid followed the original model, and the front of the building was opened so it could hold more people comfortably. This change was detrimental to the palace, which had been seriously damaged during a bombardment at the time of a siege to which the Caliph Amin was subjected. The minaret of the mosque had been destroyed by fire in 915 and was later rebuilt. This venerable sanctuary has to the present time withstood all disasters, including the Mongol conquest.

All around the main central square were the houses of Mansur's young children and his personal black slaves, the treasury, the public kitchens, the arsenal, and the offices of the Ministry of Correspondence and Land Taxes, of the Keeper of the Seal, of palace personnel, and of the Finance Ministry.

From one end of the city to the other there were alleys and streets bearing the names of officers, the caliph's protégés, or even local inhabitants. In each of them dwelled high-ranking officers in whom the caliph had a great deal of faith, his most important freedmen, and public servants who were on call in case of emergency. Solid gates closed off the ends of the streets. Except for the four main avenues, no artery ran to the wall surrounding the main, or palace, square, since all other streets and the wall were concentric.

It has been impossible to locate this early center of Baghdad, this round city, on the site itself, and there is no way even to draw up a hypothetical plan.

Baghdad was at first a fortified city inside a rampart, a large palatine city. Even the sites set aside for market places were eliminated for security reasons. Later the outlying parts of the city were divided into four sections separated by the city gates, and an engineer was engaged to lay out each section. He was told how much land to allow for market places in each, and how great an area to allocate each concession-holder.

The instructions were to reserve large sites for stores and shops and to plan for a general market in each section to handle various commercial articles. As much room was to be reserved for streets and alleys as for buildings. Avenues were seventy-eight feet wide, and streets were twenty-six feet wide. The number of neighborhood mosques and baths was to depend on population density. The engineer was ordered to take a set amount of land from the officers' and troops' concessions for the use of merchants, as well as for small retailers and foreigners, who were obliged to build their homes and live there.

Because of such planning, the activities in these neighborhoods ran smoothly and harmoniously. Unoccupied land was turned into orchards or was cultivated in order that the inhabitants would not be too crowded. A variety of crops ensured harvests in all seasons. Noisy or malodorous facilities, such as camel stables, were set up in outlying areas.

Thanks to the geographer Ya'qubi, we have the complete list of concessions, which, of course, is too long to be repeated here. The general idea was to allot sections of the city to homogeneous groups. Although this made surveillance easier, it did nothing to lessen hostility among clans.

Enumeration of the peripheral neighborhoods will help give a better idea of the development of the suburbs closest to the city. Taking the course of the Tigris as a point of departure, we find Rusafa, flanked on the northeast by Shammasiya. These two neighborhoods were separated from each other by the main avenue which started at Bab al-Taq, the Arcade Gate near Ya'qubi's main bridge, and which ran to the Shammasiya Gate. A long boulevard separated this northern group of neighborhoods from those to the south, and it too began at Bab al-Taq and ran far to the east to the Khurasan Gate. To the south of this street was the Mukharrim neighborhood, which gained renown as the site of the caliph's luxurious palaces after the beginning of Mamun's reign. Across the Tigris, to the south of the city, were the Karkh and Muhawwal neighborhoods. Muhawwal was to become a resort. Because of its many trees and streams, it resembled Ghuta in the Damascus suburbs. Harbiya, situated to the north of the Syrian Gate on the banks of the Tigris, was in ruins by the thirteenth century.

Thus, from the beginning, the city stretched out on both banks of the Tigris. The great amount of traffic between the two banks makes it important to determine the number and the locations of the pontoon bridges which were the means of communication. Louis Massignon's remark points out the difficulty of this task: "If the question of the bridges of Baghdad was definitely answered, there would be a solid basis for determining all the topography of the two banks. Unfortunately, historical texts tell us in a confused way of temporary, special bridges answering a passing need or a prince's whim, and of modifications to ordinary service bridges used for commercial purposes and the movement of the local population."

It seems that there were four or five bridges up to the reign of Mamun and only three after that.

The bridges were, of course, the nerve centers of the city, especially during battles and uprisings. Since they were very busy places, the bodies of distinguished people who had been executed were exposed on them. For example, the bodies of the members of the Barmekid family were placed in the middle of each of the bridges. Sometimes the heads of rebels were accorded this sign of public infamy.

The Upper Bridge joined Shammasiya and Rusafa to the right bank and went on to the Harbiya section and the Syrian Gate. It is mentioned in accounts of the sieges of 814 and 865, at which time it was damaged. It was composed of twenty pontoons. In 896, perhaps under the weight of too many people, part of it collapsed and one thousand persons drowned. A little later it burned, but was rebuilt under the first Buyids, who, from the time of their arrival, lived in palaces in Shammasiya. A wealthy private citizen provided money for its reconstruction. The Upper Bridge seems to have disappeared finally in the middle of the tenth century, since Istakhri and Ibn Hawqal mention only two bridges. Ibn Hawqal's text remains rather mysterious: "The two banks are today joined by a bridge at the end of Bab al-Taq; there were formerly two, but because of the small number of users, one of them, in need of repairs, has been closed to traffic."

The western sector, near the Khurasan Gate, was very close to the Tigris, along which an avenue ran. The Main Bridge crossed over to the east bank and ended near Bab al-Taq almost opposite the Palace of Eternity. The arcade (Taq), all that remained of a palace that had existed in the time of Mansur, was an outstanding landmark in the Middle Ages because of its location near a pontoon bridge. For a while the bridge was divided to provide two one-way lanes.

The Lower Bridge was called by Ya'qubi the New Bridge. It was built by order of Mansur and ran from the Barley Gate on the right bank of the Tigris to the Tuesday Market on the other side.

The Baghdad historian Khatib mentions only the Main and Lower Bridges. The Lower Bridge did not always remain in a fixed place.

When the Tigris was not raging, there were ships of many kinds on the river. Arab writers liked to name them all from the lowliest to the most fabulous ones used by the aristocracy of the city. In order to let the boats pass, some of the bridge pontoons had to be removed.

The Karkh neighborhood, famous later for its restiveness, was in the southern section, between the Kufa and the Basra Gates. It was furrowed by a system of concentric canals, the

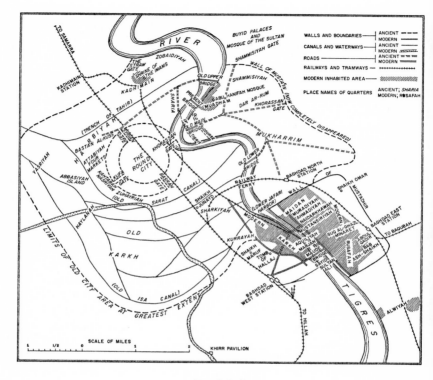

Baghdad

Adapted from a map in Richard Coke,
Baghdad the City of Peace

most important of which joined the Euphrates and the Tigris. The Sarat was the most important canal and was closest to the Round City. It flowed from the Tigris north of the Sharqiya (Eastern) district and ran toward the west through Muhawwal. Sharqiya was a very busy commercial center. There was a market here with rows of shops in which all sorts of products were sold. There were also about one hundred bookshops. It was in a Sharqiya mosque that the Friday sermons were delivered. The name Sharqiya disappeared and was replaced by the name of the Basra Gate neighborhood. The controversies between it and Karkh were a subject frequently mentioned in the chronicles.

Karkh deserves mention because of its favorable location on a knoll which was not always reached by the periodic overflowing of the Tigris. The Arab name comes from an Aramaic word meaning "fortified city." This section was the most important commercial center. The following anecdote explains why the markets were installed in the southern sector. Mansur had already reserved for the merchants the arcades in the Round City near the gates. One day he received a Byzantine ambassador and in showing him through the city asked, "How do you like it?"

"It is certainly a well planned city," said the visitor, "except for one thing. An enemy can cross it at will and without your knowledge. All your secrets will be spread throughout the world without your being able to hide them. For the markets are inside the city; they are open to everyone. The enemy will enter using business as a pretext. Besides, the merchants will travel about and will be able to talk of your most secret affairs."

That was all that was needed to move the main markets to Karkh as early as the year 774.

At the entrance to Karkh were the merchants who sold

cloth and all sorts of clothing imported from Khurasan. But most of the neighborhood consisted of a very large and continuous maze of shops and outdoor stands. Each type of business had its own fixed street with a set number of commercial locations so that the professions and various types of commerce were not mixed. No article was put on sale nor was any craft practiced outside its designated location. Each market was set up as a separate entity. Butchers, those "people totally lacking education who always have a knife in their hands," were completely isolated. They even had a mosque assigned to them in the neighborhood to keep them from entering the center of the city. There were also cloth merchants, soap dealers, and cook-shop owners. In the southern part of the district flowed the Canal of the Chickens, so named because of a large chicken market. In the same part of Karkh there was the Street of the Fullers. At the other end, toward the entrance to Muhawwal and in the direction of the Tigris, were open markets that were stocked with all sorts of merchandise.

It is rather difficult to locate precisely the Market of Thirst, which hurt Karkh with its competition soon after the Caliph Mahdi set up some retailers there. It is rather vaguely thought that it was in the vicinity of Bab al-Taq, even the name of which was unknown to Ya'qubi.

Of course, the goods found in certain markets, especially those in which a little of everything was sold, depended on the character of the people among whom they were established. Shops were even huddled together inside the walls of the caliph's palaces. Their owners practiced noble trades and furnished the needs of the court. They were the flower and fruit merchants, the goldsmiths, money-changers, and the inevitable armorers.

North of the Round City, beyond the Syrian Gate, were

markets where all sorts of products and staples were sold. This well-stocked commercial center, which branched out in several directions and joined the Harbiya sector, had avenues, streets, and courtyards. Ya'qubi states that in his time there was no neighborhood which was bigger, more important, or better provided with streets and markets. He adds that most of the residents were originally from central Asia.

There was a smaller neighborhood between the surrounding wall and the Tigris. Here were the caliph's stables, the drill field, and the Khuld (Eternity) Palace, which faced the Tigris. Mansur lived there, and so did Mahdi before he moved to the Rusafa Palace. Police headquarters and the repair shop for the pontoon bridges were located on this same bank of the Tigris, and the straw merchants also gathered in this area.

Ya'qubi's statistics for the city and its suburbs should be taken with a degree of skepticism. Ya'qubi said that there were six thousand streets and alleys, thirty thousand places of worship, and ten thousand bathhouses. These figures are certainly grossly exaggerated, as are those of other Arab writers. The markets and the shops were taxed for the first time under Mahdi's reign and must have brought to the treasury more than the equivalent of $1,400,000.

Mention has been made of the partly navigable system of canals in the southern suburb which connected the Tigris and Euphrates. They in no way hindered the movement of pedestrians, since they were spanned by arched bridges. The Karkhaya Canal, running from the Euphrates, flowed through solidly vaulted underground tunnels with bottoms made of quicklime and carefully laid baked bricks. This canal provided water to most of the neighboring streets in winter as well as in summer, since a technique had been

devised to prevent any halt in the flow. Another canal along
the same system, running from the Tigris, was named Little
Tigris (Dujail) by the caliph. Its two branches, one of
which was called the Canal of the Chickens, brought drinking water to the inhabitants of Karkh and the neighboring
area. The residents of Karkh were also supplied by the large
Isa Canal, which bordered the area to the south. It was
navigable, and large ships coming from Raqqa in Upper
Mesopotamia brought wheat and a variety of merchandise
from Syria and Egypt. They were unloaded in an uninterrupted flow in the lower port, where warehouses had been
built. This canal assured Baghdad of a ranking commercial
position. The canals also offered a fine line of defense for the
city. They were therefore indispensable, and their main-
tenance was essential. Not much information is available
about their construction and upkeep, except for the important repairs during the Buyid period.

The inhabitants of Baghdad also had wells which were
fed by the canals. As a result, the entire population drank
fresh water. Between the Basra Gate and the Khurasan Gate,
in the section of the Round City closest to the Tigris, was a
thoroughfare called the Street of the Water Carriers.

The entire area was prosperous. Trees, especially palms
brought from Basra, were planted, and Baghdad had more
palm trees than Basra or Kufa. Magnificent fruit was grown,
and there were many orchards and gardens throughout the
suburb. This is what greater Baghdad was like, with its
Round City and its suburbs, the most famous of which was
Karkh: "Everything that was manufactured in the other
countries was made here, because artisans had emigrated
from every point on the horizon; they had come as quickly
as they could from near and far."

On the outskirts of the city, in every direction, were cemeteries.

In 768 the caliph Mansur began to build another section of the city on the east bank, in a bend of the Tigris northeast of the Khurasan Gate. At first it was called Mahdi's Camp and later, Rusafa. This community was passed on to the future caliph Mahdi. According to its founder's plan, it was to be an outer defense of the capital and was therefore surrounded by a wall and a moat. A palace surrounded by gardens and a cathedral mosque were built there. The site of the mosque can be approximated because the tomb of Abu Hanifa, who was buried near by, is still in existence. This section, in which a canal was dug, was connected to the western bank by two pontoon bridges. Mansur distributed concessions in this district to his brothers and his officers.

Ya'qubi writes, "People greatly desired to live near Mahdi because he was popular." Mahdi did not permit buildings to be constructed that were too spacious. Space was set aside for a large market where all sorts of merchandise, food products, and manufactured goods were sold. To the southeast of this neighborhood was the Market of Thirst, but the attempt to attract the merchants of Karkh to this market ended in failure. Five main streets crossed this section of Baghdad.

Actually, from the time of the construction of Rusafa, the Round City ceased to exist. All the caliphs from Mahdi to Mu'tasim lived on occasion in Mahdi's Palace in Rusafa.

There was a definite reason for the establishment of Mahdi's Camp. The sovereign hoped for peace and quiet. Mansur was advised to have Mahdi and some of the troops live on the east bank.

Karkh and Rusafa are names that are still in use. The

entire left bank of the Tigris is called Karkh; Rusafa is the name of that part of Baghdad which is on the right bank. The original Rusafa fell into ruins at the time of Yaqut. Nothing was left but the mosque, which was destroyed during the Mongol conquest, the mausoleums of the Abbasid caliphs, and the tomb of Abu Hanifa. Rusafa began at the Shammasiya Gate. A road, called the Grand Avenue, ran from this gate to the neighborhood of the caliph's palaces in the south.

In addition to the Palace of the Golden Gate and the one at Rusafa, there were many other royal residences. All have disappeared, but we know approximately where they were located. In 775, the caliph Mansur had another palace built on the west bank of the Tigris, outside the ramparts, facing the Khurasan Gate. It was called Khuld (Eternity) and was used by various caliphs up to the time of Mu'tamid. According to an Arab historian, the comparison with Paradise was well founded. The panorama was splendid; the palace itself was amazingly luxurious and surprisingly well planned. Although the caliph Harun al-Rashid preferred staying in Raqqa, in Upper Mesopotamia, rather than in Baghdad, Raqqa was but a vacation spot for him; his real residence was the Palace of Eternity. That is where his harem and his children were housed and where his public treasury was located. The caliph Amin lived there, but he stayed at the Golden Gate during the siege laid down by his brother Mamun's army. Khuld remained the name of this section of the city.

The palaces of the caliphs were on the east bank of the river. Mention should be made of the mansion of the Barmecide vizier, Ja'far ibn Yahya, who liked to drink and surround himself with musicians and singers. Unable to change his son's ways, Yahya ordered him to build an out-of-the-way, isolated palace on the east bank where he could invite his fellow roisterers to revelries that at least were hidden. So it happened that Ja'far built a mansion that was to become the center of a group of palaces of the caliphate. Fantastic amounts of money were poured into the luxurious residence. The building became the property of Mamun, who moved into it before becoming caliph. He set aside neighboring land for a race track, a polo ground, and a zoo. Toward the east, a gate opened on the surrounding plain, and a canal was dug to supply water to the property. The grounds were bordered on the north by what was called, in Yaqut's time, the Main Boulevard. The building became the property of the caliph's minister, Hasan ibn Sahl. When Hasan's daughter, Buran, married Mamun, the caliph lived in the Palace of Eternity. After Hasan's death, the palace became one of Buran's possessions. Its name, Qasr Hasani, Hasan's Palace, was retained, however, in memory of Mamun's father-in-law.

The caliph Mu'tadid, the first to come back to Baghdad after this decline, increased and beautified the surrounding property, bought near-by lands, modernized them, and notably, had the race track moved farther east. The palace named the Crown (Taj) was then founded near the Tigris, and it was protected from the river's wrath by a masonry dike. The building had a cupola and was surrounded by fields and a zoological park. The cupola was called the Dome of the Donkey, because, in order to get to it, one had to ride a little gray donkey up a gently sloping ramp. This cupola was destroyed by lightning in 1154. The caliphs Muqtafi and Mustadi had it rebuilt, but with inferior materials. The caliph Qahir was besieged in the Crown Palace, which seems to have been destroyed at a later date.

The caliph Mu'tadid had thought of moving into the

Crown Palace even before it was completed. In any event, his son Muktah finished the Taj according to plan. Its main façade had five arcades which were supported by six columns. Dominique Sourdel wrote: "A place was set aside for solemn audiences. At the rear of a sort of niche, the caliph appeared to all those present; they were lined up to the right and the left of a long room and stood silent."

Mu'tadid thought of leaving the Crown Palace, because he was annoyed by the smoke of near-by houses. In the suburbs two miles to the east, he built the Palace of the Pleiades and had it connected to the other palace by an underground tunnel, which was blocked with the first flooding of the Tigris. The Pleiades received its water supply from the Musa Canal. The outlying buildings and lands stretched toward the east for several miles. A game reserve was set aside in which wild boar was hunted. This palace, of which Ibn Mu'tazz sang in his poetry, was destroyed in 1074 by a terrible flood.

The royal hunt amounted to an easy massacre with almost no human danger involved. Apparently the game was killed with the least amount of effort. It was a very elegant sport, demanding preparations as detailed as those of a military campaign, and it could, like polo, be used as a type of army training. The caliphs had had a long wall erected around the Palace of the Pleiades. The game, surrounded by this wall, was easily seen and killed by the caliph and his guests. The hunters were accompanied by servants armed with javelins and boar-spears, by huntsmen and falconers, and by horsemen with trained cheetahs. Of course this type of hunt could be risky when big game was involved. These battues were the occasion for exploits that the poets could sing about.

Another palace, al-Firdaus (meaning Paradise) was founded toward the south on the banks of the Tigris, near the Tuesday Market. It too was connected to the Pleiades by underground passageways.

On the other side of the perimeter of the caliphs' castles, Mu'tasim had a palace built near the Khurasan Gate, which was in the wall on the east bank. He lived there until his departure for Samarra.

It is evident that each caliph tried to beautify this group of palaces, and we shall see the result later with the description of Muqtadir's reception of a Byzantine ambassador. It is useless to list all the luxurious buildings which added to the beauty of these residences, which eventually became an independent, walled part of the city, called Mukharrim.

The group of palaces was known as Dar al-khilafa, the Residence of the Caliphate, and it consisted of buildings, gardens, shaded lawns, columned porticoes, and streams that ran into little lakes, all of which was enclosed by a wall in 1095. At this time the area was still called the *Harim*, meaning reserved enclosure, and was as large as the city of Shiraz, according to contemporary writers. The rampart, which was not very imposing, ran around the area in a half-circle, the ends of which were connected by the Tigris. It had a number of gates, whose names are given us by Ya'qubi. Starting at the northwest and moving east, we find the al-Gharaba Gate and the very high Gate of the Date Market, destroyed at the beginning of Nasir's reign. Then there was the Badr Gate (also called the Private Gate), named after a commander of Mu'tadid's troops. This gate was walled up around 970. Then came the Gate of the Nubian, which we shall encounter again during the Crusades. This was also called the Gate of the Threshold and was kissed by princes and ambassadors as they entered Baghdad. An iron harpoon hung from the People's Gate, where executions took place. This gate, facing toward the east, was also called the Ammuriya Gate, since it was brought from Ammuriya, after the city's conquest by the caliph Mu'tasim. A mile away, there was another gate which opened on the plain and where sacrificial animals were slaughtered. Finally, to the south, moving toward the Tigris, was the Gate of the Steps, which from the river was twice the distance of the flight of an arrow.

A long thoroughfare called Grand Avenue ran from the southern pontoon bridge to the Bab al-Taq, where there was an important junction. One road ran to the Khurasan Gate to the east, and Grand Avenue went on to the north to the Shammasiya Gate. To the west of Grand, a vast garden, the Zahir, which belonged to the caliphs, reached as far as the Tigris. An extension of Grand ran east to the Horse Market Gate. Another street, whose point of origin and terminal point are not known exactly, may have run from the Bab al-Taq to the Horse Market Gate.

Little by little, the invasion of the stronghold by markets and private residences limited the part reserved for the palaces of the caliphs.

In the year 902, the caliph Muktafi built the cathedral mosque, called the palace mosque (Jami' al-Qasr) because it was close to the Hasani Palace immediately to the east near the Tigris. This was the third place of worship built for Friday prayers, the fourth if the mosque in the Harbiya district is counted. Sermons were not always a part of the service in this mosque.

Thus, thanks to Ya'qubi, we can determine Mansur's plan of Baghdad, which was divided into districts, markets, streets, and neighborhoods on the west bank of the Tigris where the actual city and Karkh were found and on the east bank where Rusafa, formerly called the Camp of Mahdi, was built.

3.

THE TWO CENTERS OF GOVERNMENT

DELVING INTO THE HISTORY of the city of Baghdad means being interested as well in the chronicle of a dynasty, since the city was founded by the second Abbasid and was nearly totally destroyed at the time the family disappeared in Mesopotamia. We, of course, do not intend to write once again the annals of the Moslem world, but in studying the history of Baghdad and in noting its vicissitudes, we shall watch the empire of the caliphs shrink.

In addition, since there is no municipal authority to deal with, and since the political power of the caliph, or of his recognized representatives, is the only power, we cannot help but relate the events that had great influence on the inhabitants of the city. This will also be true of the Qarmatian movement and the arrival of the Seljuks, which we shall mention as a case in point.

In the same way, we shall not be able to pass over the lessening, throughout the ages, of Baghdad's political power, if only in respect to the extent of her territories.

Moving the capital from Damascus to Baghdad doomed the centralization of the empire to complete failure, since the move prevented the caliphate from continuing to play a political role in the Mediterranean. The immediate consequence was that Islamized Spain and North Africa sought autonomy within the framework of the original institutions. It is therefore in the West that dissidence first occurred, and there was a scission between the Eastern and Western empires, with each going its own way.

The eastern borderlands followed in like manner in order to satisfy the personal ambitions of those lords who had a certain degree of influence. These dynasties were Iranian, with an equal number of rabble and aristocrats, Tahirids, Saffarids, Samanids, Buyids, or Turks, Ghaznavids, and Seljuks. Their domains varied and their power was more or less ephemeral, but it is important to remember that everywhere the methods of governing were Iranian.

From the beginning, the Abbasids, for better or worse, had stopped worrying about Arab opinion. Conquered Persia had to educate the conquerors. The Abbasid administration owed everything to Persia, including court etiquette and the manners of the bourgeoisie. The numerous semi-religious, semi-political sects were especially inspired by old Iranian beliefs. Arab writers themselves recognized the influence of the past. When speaking of the investiture ceremony of the caliph, Ibn Khaldun does not hesitate to say that the ground in front of the caliph was kissed in accordance with protocol of the Sassanian court.

Thus there was in Baghdad a Persian party represented by a family of valorous men, the Barmekids, and after them came the vizier Fadl ibn Sahl, who used all his authority to back Mamun against his brother Amin.

The Barmekids entered Moslem history as prime ministers or viziers to the caliphs. We begin to see the developing concept of temporal power in the person of an administrative assistant to the caliph, while the caliph himself rises little by little from the rank of active head of all believers to that of supreme pontiff, on his way to becoming a monarch by divine right.

The reign of Harun al-Rashid marks one of the high points of the Abbasid caliphate. He was the first sovereign to live in great luxury; his popularity in Europe was magnified by *The Thousand and One Nights*. Because of the work of his predecessors, his life was free of the cares that normally accompany power. In France he is known because of his relationship with Charlemagne, which remains somewhat mysterious. Arab historians do not speak about it, probably because the ambassadors left from the Aghlabid principality and not from Baghdad. We rely on the authenticity of Eginhard's account written at the time.

It would be difficult to defend Amin, who is described as an intemperate debauché. He spent his days with his precious men friends, in spite of his mother's efforts to cure him by dressing pretty young girls as pages. It seems to us that he gave proof of an unaccountable lack of political comprehension when he defied his father's will, which had provided for the future succession to power of his brother Mamun.

The succession of Harun al-Rashid therefore marks the beginning of a violent crisis brought on by a brutally significant event, the struggle between the dead caliph's two sons. Amin, of purely Arab ancestry, was attacked in his capital by the troops of Mamun, the son of an Iranian woman.

As soon as it was officially announced that Amin had repudiated his father's will, an army left Khurasan and rushed toward Baghdad. The hostilities lasted fourteen months, the people of the city seeking protection as best they could. The mosques were deserted, and public prayers were abandoned. The battle grew more and more fierce. The caliph Amin was at first held in check in his castle in the Round City on the west bank of the Tigris. He later shut himself up in the Khuld Palace. The people of Baghdad split into two camps, and an all-out deadly battle took place in a neighborhood of the west city. The streets and alleys were strewn with bodies. Under the command of Tahir, Mamun's general, war machines hurled their projectiles against the city, causing destruction everywhere. Fire increased the damage. It is impossible to imagine how great the ruin was during these unforgettable days. Only the Karkh neighborhood seems not to have suffered too greatly.

Soon the caliph Amin was surrounded only by ragged, poorly armed soldiers. Claude Cahen says, "In pages that deserve to be classified among the classics of all peoples, Tabari and Mas'udi described the battle of these naked men, who, with only sticks and stones as weapons and palm leaves as shields, fought off the heavy charging horsemen until the fierce and inevitable final slaughter."

For the first time, mention is made, among the ranks of the defenders of the caliph Amin, of the famous *ayyar*, who were talked about for more than four centuries. The *ayyar* corporation brings to mind the "idea of a wandering existence outside the framework of laws and society," held together by group solidarity. These people were similar to the vagrants of our Middle Ages, to present-day mercenaries, and to unscrupulous individuals who are pretentious enough to want to control everything. In examining certain contemporary attitudes more closely, we cannot help but think of the violent opposition of the materially disinherited to those who are more fortunate. It would be as easy as it is false to speak of bandits and criminals; categorizing them is much more complex. Our informants, the historians, are members of the professorial bourgeoisie, and their hostility is quite understandable. The plebeian origin of the group is certain. A conclusive example is the career of Saffar, who

CHECKED BY _____

PJ7715 Arabian Nights
B8   Richard Burton

V1
P.3 - 3 days + the storm of the guest - site
      Eroes ground plum. hands for king

P.4 violence - killing for adultry

P.5 aberrito

P.6 much deal women attracted sexually
     to negroes bro. of size

P.7 malice of women

P.8 carpet-bed

was the chief of an *ayyar* band before founding a powerful dynasty that made Persia and Mesopotamia tremble.

In any event, the *ayyar* had good officers and leaders bearing military titles. A passage by the annalist Ibn al-Athir deals with a later period but still is enlightening: "Baghdad was the scene of a serious uprising during which the caste mentality persisted at the very time the population was called upon to take sides. The *ayyar* openly sowed disorder and attacked certain properties. It was the unchaining of a fanaticized population brandishing all sorts of weapons, swords, lances, bows, and even cutlasses. Many secret meetings had taken place. From these came family groups, associations of *futuwwa*, Sunnite and Shi'ite partisans, and the *ayyar*. From then on there were pillage, murder, and arson."

It is impossible to write a social history of Baghdad without mentioning the *ayyar*, those vagabonds in the grand manner who in Aleppo and Damascus were called *ahdath*. We should not think that the historian Mas'udi is guilty of an anachronism when he speaks of the *ayyar* at the time of the siege of Amin, nor should we exaggerate the Qarmatian influence on the movement. At the very least, the Qarmatian organization could have maintained a certain amount of discipline over these agitators.

Let us return to Baghdad's battle with Mamun's army. As the commander tightened the siege and neighborhood after neighborhood fell, the people came to his aid. Finally the Khurasan general, annoyed by the faithfulness of Amin's partisans despite the destruction, fire, and carnage caused by his siege machines, cut off supplies coming by way of Basra, Wasit, and other routes. The caliph's situation became critical; he now held only small parts of the old city. Preparing to flee, he was betrayed by a groom, who beheaded him.

This is how the reign of Mamun came about. One detail

35

is rather picturesque. It took a rebellion in Baghdad for Mamun to give up Merv as the seat of the Moslem empire. Did Mamun declare the Alid Ali Rida heir apparent in order to satisfy part of Persian public opinion? It is rather difficult to untangle the reasons for what is called "collusion between Iranianism and Shi'ism." This determination gave rise to repercussions in Baghdad which became even more serious, with Mamun's insistence that he would not leave Khurasan. Barbier de Meynard has described with much wit and knowledge the accession to the throne of an uncle of Mamun's, Ibrahim ibn Muhdi, rightly more famous as a musician and singer than as an ephemeral caliph whose reign lasted just less than two years. This period was just long enough for Mamun to decide to go back to Baghdad, and Ali Rida died mysteriously.

During a century and a half of Abbasid power, there was periodic repression of opposing Alids. Each caliph had an Alid that he had to put down with merciless force. The Alids had a growing feeling of frustration at the time of the disappearance of the Umayyads. The messianic role to be played so ably by the Qarmatians and the Fatimids can already be seen. The caliph Mamun's proclamation making Ali Rida heir apparent could have been a political act "destined to avoid the worst." In any event, it caused a scission between the Shi'ites and the Sunnites. Panic stricken, the Sunnites saw in the proclamation pseudo-recognition of Alid legitimacy.

Under Mamun, the Persians enjoyed a certain amount of autonomy. One of the men who was responsible for the caliph's success took advantage of the situation. He was a member of the Tahirid family, whose diplomatic position is not too clear. The caliph considered the Tahirids governors, but with the right of hereditary succession. Harun al-Rashid had inaugurated this policy in North Africa for the Aghlabids.

The year 936 was marked by very serious incidents. Brigands from the Harbiya district, joined by bands of thieves from the city itself and from the Karkh suburb, engaged in horrible crimes against the people. They shamelessly plundered, robbed, pillaged, and carried off pages and women. No one could stop them; they demanded money from passersby, they invaded the surrounding towns, encircled houses, and took movable objects and money. Since they served as a force supporting the men in power, no authority opposed them. Thinking they were beyond restriction, they attacked people walking in the streets and the parks and held them for ransom. This was a terrible catastrophe for the inhabitants of Baghdad. The village of Qatrabbul, in the northern suburbs, was pillaged, but the bandits were not satisfied with merely stealing furniture. They carried off sheep, donkeys, and cattle. Powerless to do anything, the owners complained in vain to the authorities. Finally, one brave man, who knew how to lead, organized neighborhood groups, called the Volunteers, which finally re-established order. The brigands were hunted down, and many of them were killed in the streets, the market places, and the suburbs. Money was distributed to help bring about peace. The Volunteers had first appeared about the time that Ibrahim ibn Mahdi came to the throne several years before. Mas'udi considers them vicious individuals supported by the dregs of society. They bring to mind the *ayyar*.

Although the foregoing is a description of what occurred in Baghdad, the situation was the same throughout Persia and Mesopotamia. Jahiz mentions similar incidents in Basra, and the following remark by Muqaddasi about Shiraz is revealing: "The mosque in this city is always full of brigands, scoundrels, and people without either faith or law who make it their headquarters and their meeting place."

Thus, as it is chronicled, in Baghdad the thieves were organized in a corporation and their activities continued into the following century. Mas'udi has some curious revelations: "The *repentants* are old thieves of all categories who, as they grew older, renounced their trade; when a crime is committed, they know who the guilty person is and have him tracked down. However, at times, they also split the take with the thief. Their agents are spread out in the neighborhoods and the streets, in the inns, the taverns, the food shops, and the gambling houses."

There was an evil side to the reign of Mamun and his two successors, which should not be hidden. This was the imposition upon the people, through frightful persecution, of the Mutazilite doctrine, which though finally defeated might have won out through peaceful preaching. It was an aloof movement of intellectual independence, which was grave and austere, favored free will, and appealed to reason with logical arguments. Its conclusions, dominated by the idea of God's extreme justice, were comforting. Its thesis concerning the origin of the Koran made it unpopular, since the holy book lost its essential quality of being the word of God. Baghdad played a capital role in this movement, a fact that pays tribute to the intelligence of the free-thinkers of the time. In religious circles, the obstinacy of Ibn Hanbal, who preferred imprisonment to adherence to Mutazilite doctrines, was never forgotten.

In his zealous pursuit of non-Moslems and Shi'ites, the caliph Mutawakkil, who had thought of making Damascus capital of the empire once again, was merely following established methods; he had simply changed the target. When he attacked the tomb of Husain, the son of the caliph Ali, in

851, the people answered with a poster campaign. The caliph was cursed in writing on the walls of private homes and mosques. But every trace of the tomb had completely disappeared.

The people of Baghdad soon witnessed another spectacle. Fifty years after the dynasty had begun, the character of the army changed because of the constant influx of Turkish mercenaries, recruited in central Asia from the time of the reign of Mu'tasim, Harun al-Rashid's second son, who had succeeded his brother Mamun. Higher ranks were open to these Turks even during the lifetime of Mu'tasim, who distinguished them from the other troops by splendid uniforms enhanced by brocade, swordbelts, and gilt ornaments. The great historian Ibn Khaldun lashes out at them: "Men have been able to consent to entering the state of servitude, but this has been with the hope of attaining honor, riches, and power; such were the Turks in the service of the Abbasid caliphs."

During the reign of Mamun, his brother Mu'tasim sent missions to the Samanids to buy Turkish slaves at Samarkand. Each year he was sent a certain number until there was a collection of three thousand pages. When Mu'tasim became caliph, he stubbornly continued this recruitment and even bought slaves who were already privately owned in Baghdad, thus acquiring great numbers of them.

At first the Turks were not required to convert to Islam. A writer, who witnessed their stationing in Baghdad, stated: "When the pagan Turks rode their horses through the city, they rushed forward striking left and right to move the crowd back. Sometimes, when they were attacked by the people, they wounded individuals and committed murder. Blood was shed with impunity, and the authors of these crimes were never bothered."

The arrival of the Turkish mercenaries in the caliph's

capital indicated that the caliph was beginning to distrust the Khurasanians and also that this could have been a way to loosen the Iranian hold. But another danger arose with the disorders in the city caused by these soldiers.

In order to protect the lives of his Turkish guards, the caliph, who at first lived in his brother Mamun's palace, had a new mansion built on the east bank of the river and thought of building billets for the guards at Shammasiya, a district that was at that time separated from the city of Baghdad itself. But the latter site seemed too close and too narrow. He therefore chose a place about sixty miles to the north of Baghdad, on the plain where Samarra was to be built. Protection of the Turkish guards was ostensibly the reason for moving them, but later chronicles tell how much the inhabitants of Baghdad suffered because of the attitude of the Turks, who plundered private homes and attacked women. A great number of murders were committed each day. It is said that the caliph Mu'tasim, the builder of Samarra, made this characteristic statement: "If the troops of Baghdad were to cause trouble, I myself would be protected and I would be able to attack them by land and by sea."

Samarra, that palatine city called in the West the Versailles or the Windsor Castle of the caliphate, assumed exceptional importance in the history of art. It served as the residence of eight caliphs, all of whom quickly realized that they had created their own masters. These praetorians proved unbearable. They made and unmade caliphs at will, without even respecting their persons. It is obvious, then, that the massive introduction of Turkish soldiers into the caliph's army marks the beginning of the decline of the Abbasid caliphate.

The turbulence of the inhabitants of Baghdad and of Iraq in general must have been a dangerous reality for the caliphs to have thought it necessary that they be protected by foreign mercenaries. It must have been difficult to find a balance between the caliph, the Turks who watched over him, and the city dwellers who were far from calm.

The building of Samarra constitutes an attempt to abandon Mansur's old city. The methods used by the founder of the Abbasid capital were an inspiration to the builders of the new city. Ya'qubi says: "The prosperity of Baghdad did not suffer by it. Its markets did not lose any of their importance, because they could not be replaced and because, in addition, buildings and homes were being constructed constantly between Baghdad and Samarra, in the interior as well as along the river; I am referring to the Tigris and its banks."

A passage by the same author informs us of the later activity of the artisans in Lower Mesopotamia. "The caliph Mu'tasim gave a written order to bring in workers, masons, specialists, blacksmiths, carpenters, and other artisans, and to transport all sorts of wood, especially teak, palmtree trunks from Basra and its surroundings, from Baghdad and its neighborhood, from Antioch, and from all the Syrian coast. He also sent for marble-cutting and laying specialists, and in Latakia and other cities marble workshops were established. From everywhere, he also called for artisans of all kinds, able construction workers, gardeners who knew how to sow, plant, and arrange palm groves, engineers expert in the art of distributing and measuring water and of tapping streams and discovering them. It is thus that he sent to Egypt for papyrus makers, among others, to Basra for glassmakers, potters, and straw braiders, to Kufa for potters and dye makers."

From 863 on, there are records of an uprising of the military mercenaries and the reaction of the population against the Turks, whose hold on the government was criticized. They were accused of killing caliphs and of enthroning their own candidates, without regard for religion or the general interest. The murder of the caliph Mutawakkil had left a strong impression on the public, and about the same time, one of the bridges was burned and the other was cut so that its pontoons drifted downstream.

As a result, the caliphs did not live calm lives in Samarra, which remained the center of power for a little over half a century. Eight caliphs lived there, but only one episode will be mentioned here, since it takes us back to Baghdad. The caliph Musta'in decided to leave Samarra to escape the tyranny of the Turks, who proclaimed Mu'tazz caliph. The unfortunate Musta'in sought refuge in Baghdad in 865, setting up his headquarters in Rusafa. From then on, a merciless battle which raged for an entire year reduced the people of Baghdad to famine and obliged them to defend a caliph who had abdicated and was destined to be assassinated. Baghdad, still suffering from the disastrous consequences of the siege under Amin, could have done very well without the massacre, fire, and pillage that accompanied the savage fighting. The battle machines used during the siege almost entirely destroyed the Rusafa section of the city.

It was during this siege that a new outer wall was built around the Rusafa, Shammasiya, and Mukharrim sections to protect the city from the east. These ramparts are very important, since they seem to have been laid out according to a plan which coincides exactly with the one described by Ibn Jubayr and, consequently, with the modern one. The new protective measures prove that the Round City had lost its former importance.

The use of the Turks had raised a barrier between what can almost be called the spiritual power and the temporal power. In a sense, this perverted the fundamental ideas of early Islam. The Turks intended to govern, and little by little they made their purpose known to the Moslem world. They destroyed nothing; they superimposed their own authority on the existing government machinery. They kept the caliph and the vizier, who became their protégés but were pitilessly destroyed if they resisted.

4

DISILLUSIONED CALIPHS AND PALACE MAYORS

THE RELIGIOUS QUARRELS AND TROUBLES caused by the military were not the only reasons for the disintegration of the caliph's power.

The large suburbs of Baghdad were shaken by different revolutionary movements which had an influence on the behavior of the people. For two centuries the population lived in turmoil. First the caliphate had to fight a group of Gypsies who, having left India because of a famine, had settled in the Basra region. They acquired a significant amount of power and were beginning to threaten the important trade with India and China. Mu'tasim could not defeat these bandits, who fought from boats in the swamps and remained inaccessible. The caliph had the brilliant idea of using captives from the Egyptian delta against them, men who also were used to living in swamps. When the Gypsies encountered their own techniques, they were defeated in a guerrilla war.

Lower Mesopotamia became the theater of terrible slave uprisings. Zanzibar Negroes, who had worked on plantations under pitiful conditions, spread terror from Baghdad to Basra. For about fifteen years, starting with 869, they terrorized and bloodied the country. Finally, soldiers on a fleet of flatboats successfully chased the rebels into the swamps and exterminated large numbers of them.

Aside from the Turks, exactly what was the military value of what could then be called the caliph's troops? The frequent disturbances forced the authorities to take into the service mercenaries recruited from any group. Included were a band of vagrants and vagabonds who had already been enlisted during the siege of Baghbad under Amin.

The rise of the Saffarids added a new dimension to events. Their growing power was to threaten the caliph's existence. Without a doubt, the movement rose from the lower levels of society. The Saffarids used to advantage the restlessness of the people. The first band chieftain was a coppersmith. This is where the family name (Saffar) came from. After having crossed Fars and Khuzistan, the Saffarid army attacked Baghdad and was badly beaten in 879. The caliph had a narrow escape, and, in order to keep the turbulent troops away from the capital, he turned some valuable lands over to new masters, who were proving to be a threat. In the face of this uprising, the regent of the caliphate took important measures. For financial reasons or because the Saffarids did not let the convoys of Turkish slaves through, he completed his army by enlisting the lower classes of Baghdad. The Saffarids were soon to have a great impact on the ruling dynasty by showing the people how weak it was. There was a popular explosion, a gigantic tidal wave, and from then on it was obvious that Baghdad would have difficulty controlling the situation.

Although the caliphate seemed already to be falling, this was not true in the eastern provinces of Persia, where the aristocratic Samanid family permitted the nobles, who had lost their power, to regain their rights. Solidly entrenched in Khurasan, the new potentates did not directly concern the caliph of Baghdad, but they had a decisive influence on his destiny through the trade in Turkish slaves. This was at first due to the Samanids' aggressive attacks against their Turkish neighbors. Because the captives taken on the battlefield were sent to Baghdad from the time of Mamun on, the Samanids were indirectly the creators of the notorious Turkish militia.

Some idea can be gained of the crumbling of the caliph's territory at the end of the ninth century when one thinks of the provinces bordering on the Caspian Sea which were never completely subjugated.

The disorders caused by the Gypsies, followed by the social revolution of the black slaves, gave way to the sweeping charge of the Saffarids. One terrible hazard followed another for the inhabitants of Baghdad. These events were hardly finished when a formidable outbreak occurred in the area, which since the time of the Umayyads had always been a center of stubborn resistance. This time it was the Qarmatian conspiracy, whose new revolutionaries displayed a certain originality by sounding out public opinion. Missionaries tried to win popular sympathy; able emissaries mixed with the people on all levels and used religious, social, or racial arguments appropriate to the circles they were trying to propagandize. The Qarmatian crisis, the most harmful that Islam had undergone, undermined discipline and brought terror to all the Moslem East.

It is our purpose here to summarize only those facts which had moral or material repercussions on the life of Baghdad. All of Lower Mesopotamia was, in fact, laid waste. When Basra was occupied in 900, the caliph sent out an expeditionary force which was soundly beaten, and the flight of soldiers to Baghdad made a deplorable impression on the people. The caliphate, however, did not remain inactive. The army was sent to Syria when the movement suddenly started to stir up things in that country. This time the caliph won a decided victory. Qarmatian captives were sent to Baghdad, where the people were invited to witness horrible tortures inflicted on the prisoners before they were executed.

In 904, the caliph went as far as Raqqah to congratulate the victorious general. The expedition, which did not last very long, became ineffective in the face of Qarmatian activity, which, in one case in Mesopotamia, took the form of an attack on a poorly protected caravan of pilgrims. Qarmatian partisans were found even in the city and the exasperated people of Baghdad dared blame the vizier himself. The caliph's government realized that it had to do something about the thorny problem of protecting pilgrims. The minister, Ali ibn Isa, came to an agreement, which was only partially successful, with the Qarmatian leader. Military intervention was far from effective. The following complaint is found in a chronicle of the time: "The soldiers of Baghdad are like women; they eat well in their barracks, and they refresh themselves with ice and fans."

The decadence of the caliphate, which has already been touched upon, is evident in two ways: the reduction of the personal power of the caliph and the emancipation of territories which were taken over by independent princes. The people of Baghdad thus came to realize that the caliph's domain had shrunk. (For purposes of clarity, we have set up into special groups the knowledge we have about the provinces that were breaking up at that period.) The people must have been quite disturbed when they heard the curses pronounced from the pulpits against Ibn Tulun, who, obeying the caliph, escaped to Egypt. The caliph later sanctioned the autonomy of the rather ephemeral Tulunid dynasty (868–905).

The caliph, therefore, was not a strong ruler imposing

47

his will. He was not even the type of fictitious caliph whose vizier is really master. The commanders of the Turkish militia held the power. In order to justify their authority, they saw to it that they were given a new title in 908—*amir al-umara*, "emir of emirs," in imitation of the Iranian "king of kings." They were chief emirs and can be correctly compared with the Palace Mayors of Merovingian France. The post was an enviable but dangerous one, since it was that of the principal personage in a state that was breathing its last. This gave rise to intrigues that led to uprisings. There followed a series of petty rivalries, a scramble for position and honor, dominated by unsavory cliques. But even before this period, the caliph had been hardly anything but a puppet in the hands of the viziers and the Turkish officers.

The interior weakening of the caliphate was accompanied by the breaking away of territories. The tenth century was notable for the beginning of independent principalities whose rapid multiplication was not based on communal, tribal, or national feelings. Rather, it was the result of geographical necessity as well as of personal ambition.

One characteristic fact dominates the entire tenth century. Each of the great families of Islam carved out a kingdom. They seemed to want to stop the tendency toward a breakdown into smaller principalities.

A rather unexpected and moving fact should be noticed: three caliphs, representing the most important activity in the early days of Islam, divided among themselves the Moslem world. In Baghdad, the Abbasid ruler, the least independent of the three, tried to resist Shi'ite propaganda which threatened to wipe out what remained of the caliph's authority, or at least tried to stir up his subjects. He also attempted to keep a semblance of power over the holy places of Arabia, although his efforts were not always successful.

48

The Fatimids, who had just established themselves in Egypt, arrived with a will to dominate all, and that desire died only with their eventual fall. Finally, there was the Umayyad prince who reigned in Cordova and who let the Moslem world know in 929 that he too claimed the caliphate.

Seen from Mesopotamia, the situation was tragic, as reflected by the historian of the period, Mas'udi: "Today the power of Islam is weakening and declining. The Greeks are winning out over the Moslems; pilgrimages are falling into disuse; no one talks of holy wars; messages are intercepted and roads are unsafe; the different heads of Moslem countries isolate themselves and set up independent governments, and thus imitate the behavior of the satraps after Alexander's death."

It was apparent that the caliph, the supreme pontiff of Sunnism, had been reduced to governing his own palace. A single city had governed the Islamic empire, and one statement, rather than a long dissertation, is all that is needed to show how far the empire had fallen. In the first part of the tenth century, the caliph's whole territory was restricted to a single city.

We have now come to what has been justly called the Ismailian century of Islam, when the initiatory propaganda of the Qarmatian secret societies, with Kufa as their center, took hold everywhere in the western part of the empire, especially in the capital.

When the caliphate returned to Baghdad from Samarra, the authorities paid little attention to the Round City, which was completely abandoned for the east bank. Only the area around the Basra Gate remained particularly active up to the time of the Mongol conquest.

Religious disorders broke out, and adversaries, stirred to fanaticism by local leaders, fought one another in the streets and market places of Baghdad. Peace had already been disturbed by the discussions which had lined up the Mutazilites against the orthodox Sunnites. But we are referring especially to the disorders caused by the two large rival factions of Islam—the Shi'ites and the Sunnites—and, especially in the latter group, the Hanbalites.

Unfortunately, the caliph sometimes set the example. That was how Muqtadir came to attack the Shi'ites. In Baratha, a village in the western suburbs of Baghdad, were a mosque and a cemetery venerated by the Shi'ites. According to legend, the Caliph Ali had camped on that spot during his march against the Kharijites. By order of the caliph, the mosque was surrounded one Friday, all the faithful were carried off and imprisoned for a long time, and the mosque was completely destroyed. The caliph Radi had it rebuilt in 940, and public prayer was again said there the following year. The sovereign had his name engraved in the mosque, but it was no longer an Alid shrine. It became one of the capital's cathedral mosques.

Eight years later, however, the Hanbalites attacked the shrine. The caliph took personal charge. People caught on the spot were beaten with rods, and the death penalty was decreed for anyone who might attempt to damage the mosque.

Without insisting upon the fact, it is obvious that the unfortunate caliphs were now prisoners of their ministers or their mercenaries. Muqtadir's government has been harshly judged by Arab writers. They tell us that there were many uprisings during his reign because of the sovereign's youth and the power that his mother, his wives, and his eunuchs had over him. The treasury was empty, and dissension was general. Muqtadir lost his throne, was restored to it, and finally died a violent death. It is pointed out, not without irony, that the caliph's mother, grandmother, and great-grandmother had been Greek princesses. Qahir was removed from his throne and was blinded with a hot iron. The historians take pleasure in telling us that Radi, who led a happy life, was the last to have any authority at all. Then a Turkish officer, Tuzun, marched on Baghdad, which was soon abandoned by the caliph Muttaqi, who fled to Mosul. Taking advantage of the situation, the people looted his palace. The sovereign was taken in by Tuzun's promises. Muttaqi returned to Baghdad, fell into a trap, and was blinded. The same fate was in store for Mustakfi. This is the story of the years between 908 and 945. It is customary to speak of the insignificance of the caliphs, but this series of murders can prove just as easily that they did try to govern. The uprisings in the capital reached their height in the middle of the tenth century.

The following remark by Radi indicates that some of the caliphs were not lacking in foresight: "Baghdad had prestige when there were ten million dinars in the state's strongboxes. But now there is no more money, and it is like any other city." And the caliph Muti' adds to this, "All that I have is a pittance that is not even enough to take care of my needs, while the world is in the hands of the Buyid lords and the provincial governors. Neither the holy war, nor the pilgrimage, nor any other matter demanding the sovereign's attention is within my realm."

But we should consider facts that are even more tragic. As Marius Canard said, "For Baghdad, the tenth century and the beginning of the eleventh century are a period of political, religious, and social troubles that, all in all, deal a serious blow to the prosperity of the city and to its rank in the Moslem world." From 896 on, there was a growing revolt of the people against the black eunuchs; the people were whipped into submission. It would be tiresome to list the many cases of military sedition under the different reigns just reviewed. Because of their importance, however, some bear mention. For years, a segment of the population was always ready to go out into the streets whenever there was a chance they could gain something by looting. Historians tell of constant uprisings which left the city half-demolished. At the same time, soldiers and fiscal agents ruined the inhabitants.

In 918, a very rich man, Hamid ibn Abbas, became vizier. He was in the good graces of the caliph Muqtadir because of his immense fortune, but his lack of ability was notorious at the very time when Qarmatian unrest made frequent, costly expeditions necessary. This did not stop these revolutionaries from carrying on their activities. Their successes had a disastrous influence on the morale of the troops, who were not only paid poorly but were often paid quite late.

The people revolted the next year, burned the prisons, released the prisoners held under common law, and attacked and looted the building housing the police chief. The rioters, who were chased by an army detachment, sought refuge in a mosque, whereupon the caliph ordered all exits blocked and everyone arrested. Some went to prison, others had their hands chopped off.

In 921, new disorders occurred because of an increase in prices when the vizier Hamid interfered with the flow of supplies to the capital. In 924, there was sedition on the part of the military, who demanded to be paid. There was even an open battle in the streets of Baghdad between the troops of two rival officers.

It is to this caliph, Muqtadir, and to this sorry vizier, Hamid (there are people whose names should be blackened.), to this man with the "summary Sunnite faith of a jeering policeman" (as Massignon puts it) that we owe the unjust condemnation of the mystic Hallaj, who was hanged in 922 in the presence of a huge crowd after a long, diabolically planned trial. In short, the statesmen of this period did not write the most beautiful pages of Islamic history. There is no need to demonstrate their intellectual poverty and their greed. The ministers were grasping, intriguing extortioners.

Let us continue to develop our sad list of incidents which were harmful to the tranquility of the Mesopotamian capital. These are somber and monotonous annals. Between 921 and 932 eighteen uprisings were counted. During the fifteen years that followed, there were disorders involving the troops, and to these should be added the quota of Qarmatian troubles. In addition, clans were exterminating each other, and market places were being burned and looted. Even the Pleiad Palace was sacked at one time. Revolts were put down brutally. The moral climate was deplorable, especially where money was concerned. One is tempted to excuse the covetousness and the lack of discipline of the soldiers. To all this should be added the scarcity of necessities and growing tax burdens. The caliph had no solutions for the many problems which arose all at once. For example, an order was given to condemn from the pulpits the Baridite troops recruited by the tax-farmers, who had succeeded in administering Lower Mesopotamia for their own profit. But the weakness of the palace mayor, Ibn Raiq, should be noted. He granted the options of fighting the Baridites, of leaving them alone, or of concluding a treaty with them.

About the same time, there arrived in Baghdad a body of Dailamite troops, who were to serve as mercenaries to the highest bidder in the city. In some ways they were the avantgarde of the Buyid princes who were soon to place the caliphate under their protection. The troops had to be billeted separately from the Turks in order to avoid clashes. The Dailamites were no easier to control than their rivals. When they went out into the streets, they recruited partisans from among the lower classes of the capital. They attacked private property, destroyed the chain-pumps in the orchards, and looted shamelessly. In short, they caused disorder everywhere. We shall cite as a witness only one commentator of the period, Suli: "The Dailamites came down into my home from the terrace, without my being aware of it, while I was holding a literary gathering at which several men of letters were present. They left me none of my precious objects or my other movable possessions. They seized everything. They took about two hundred articles of clothing from me, which were for the most part caliphal robes coming to me as gifts from the caliphs. They also took from me precious glass and porcelain objects. They found a pack of my course notebooks, which they pillaged. Everything that they could find was carried off."

Finally, when the Dailamites settled in Baghdad after the flight of Ibn Raiq, they fomented a real insurrection, during which there was great property damage. The situation was chaotic. People fought on the side of each of the military groups—Baridite, Qarmatian, Dailamite, Turkish—and there was a general massacre. Finally, the Dailamites were chased, in turn, by the troops of the Hamdanid lord of Mosul, Nasir al-daula, who brought the caliph back to the capital and assumed the functions of palace mayor.

But, in the year 944, a historian records another grave fact: "Armed attacks became numerous. The bandits were assured of impunity by paying tribute. They assaulted passersby at night and were not even afraid to do so during the day. They got together in gangs and formed a veritable army of thieves who, at night, armed with swords and arrows, attacked the home of one person or another."

It seems that the first somewhat violent religious clashes were organized with at least the tacit consent of the caliphate. They were frequent between the years 925 and 940. On several occasions, the Hanbalites, whose severe austerity was well known, carried out punitive raids against cabarets, searched private homes, poured jars of wine into the streets, molested female slave singers and opposed their being sold, and roughed up men walking in the company of young women or ephebes. The caliph Radi, finally becoming angry, forbade these excesses, threatened the Hanbalites with his thundering fury, and warned them that he would deal with them most severely. As a matter of fact, the head of the police laid siege to a mosque in which some of these recalcitrants had sought refuge.

The upheavals troubled some sections of the city more than others, especially Karkh and its immediate surroundings. The caliph's residences, surrounded by solid walls, were left in peace. The caliph and his courtiers could carouse far from the noise of the people, among sumptuous pavilions, surrounded by splendid gardens.

The people of the capital were invited from time to time to participate in public celebrations. There was, for example, the celebration organized to honor the caliph Mu'tadid's victory in 896, a celebration which ended in tragedy. Cupolas were set up in the city and the streets were carpeted. The caliph lined up his troops in perfect battle order in front of the Shammasiya Gate, from which they marched to the Hasani Palace. Several chiefs received garments of honor and were paraded triumphantly among the people as a reward for their valorous deeds. One conquered rebel, perched atop an elephant, was dressed in a brocaded silk robe and wore a high, raw-silk bonnet. The caliph was dressed in black and wore a pointed bonnet. Crossing from one bank of the Tigris to the other, the crowd became so dense that the roadway of the bridge collapsed on a boat full of people. On the banks of the river, there were frightful shouts and cries of distress. A thousand people, not counting those who disappeared, died that day. Divers used harpoons to pull bodies out of the river.

In 918, during the reign of the mediocre sovereign Muqtadir, a Byzantine delegation, sent by the emperor Constantine Porphyrogenitus, arrived in Baghdad to negotiate a truce and to ransom prisoners. The procession entered the city on Grand Avenue, which ran on the left bank from Shammasiya Gate to the caliph's palaces. The Crown Palace was vast at that time and had a succession of open courtyards, corridors, and large audience rooms which were covered with beautiful rugs and decorated with luxurious ornaments. Chamberlains and other officers were stationed at doors, vestibules, passageways, corridors, courtyards, and rooms. The troops, in handsome uniforms, mounted on horses with gold and silver saddles, were arrayed in two columns. In front of them stood their parade horses. These soldiers lined the streets from Shammasiya Gate, in the northeast, to the caliph's palace. The markets on the west bank, the boulevards, the streets, and the terraces were crowded with people. All the shops and all the balconies had been rented for incredible sums. On the Tigris, longboats, ships, light craft, and rowboats were lined up in order and decorated with wreaths. The ambassador and his entourage paraded to the vizier's palace.

The ambassador stayed there for two months, during which time he was well entertained. He was probably invited to hunting parties on the plain between the Crown and the Pleiad palaces, which Muqtadir had set aside as a game preserve. One of the wonders shown him was the famous solid silver tree in which were perched large and small mechanical birds of various species, covered with gold and silver. Most of the tree branches were silver and some were gilded. They bent at times. They were covered with leaves of various colors which moved as though blown by the wind while each of the birds sang or cooed. Of course, there were walks through the caliph's palace, whose walls were covered with brocaded curtains superbly decorated with embroideries depicting cows, elephants, horses, camels, lions, and birds. There were also extensive draperies of solid color or with designs, and the floors were covered with expensive rugs. The ambassador was shown the zoological park, especially the collection of wild animals, among which were four elephants caparisoned in brocade and silk and about one hundred lions. The Byzantine dignitary was also taken to a kiosk between two orchards in the middle of which was a pool of mercury with four light, gilded boats decorated with gold-stitched cloth.

On one of the walls of the Tree Pavilion were pictures of fifteen horsemen dressed in brocade and other materials. In their hands they held javelins with lance heads all aimed at the same line. One cannot help but think of the famous frieze of the archers of Persepolis.

Finally, the ambassador was received in solemn audience by the caliph Muqtadir in the Crown Palace. He was even more greatly impressed because he was brought in through an underground passage. The caliph was dressed in a costume of gold Egyptian damask and wore a high headdress, and he was seated on an ebony throne covered with rich cloth. To the right of the throne were suspended nine necklaces that were in the form of rosaries, to the left seven others made of the most magnificent jewels, whose sparkle out-shone the light of day. Before the caliph stood five of his sons.

The luxury displayed on this occasion, which "marks the apogee of Abbasid splendor," showed complete disregard for the surrounding economic distress.

While on the subject of this luxurious reception, we should mention the cruel fate of Muqtadir's brother and successor, the caliph Qahir. It could be said that his wretched death was worthy of his frightful attitude during his short reign. He enjoyed shedding blood, and, as the inventor of various horrible tortures, he alienated everyone. He was attacked by his own soldiers, who tore out his eyes. He was imprisoned in the caliph's palace, which he was later obliged to leave. One day he was found dressed in rags, wearing wooden clogs, and begging for alms. It is not surprising that the Buyids had no respect for the caliph's person; there were enough precedents.

It was at this time, probably because of the very dangerous circumstances, that the urgent question of the circulation of money was resolved.

In a brilliant study, Louis Massignon has established that "the sharp demand of the farm and city workers, . . . the Qarmatian agitation . . . , for full social equality had been accelerated, if not provoked, by a concentration of two factors that led to action: a concentration of capital, thanks to the formation of a caste, first largely Christian and then Jewish, of arbitragist bankers who operated out of Baghdad, had far-off branches, and supplied the state with minted metal; and a concentration of laborers, thanks to the slave raids, or rather colonial raids subsidized by these same bankers and called holy wars, which were carried out in order to assure the permanent functioning of the workshops in the city and the work sites on the plantations."

About the same time, Jewish financiers bearing the official title of Bankers of the Court began to appear in the Abbasid capital. They guaranteed salary payments with a periodic contribution of currency, which they procured by farming out certain taxes. For the state this system was better than "borrowing from the big Baghdad merchants at a 30 per cent fee per year in order to pay the troops or to debase the currency."

We have pointed out the military difficulties in the capital and the disorders in Lower Mesopotamia without mentioning that the onrush of the Saffarids had made the Iranian roads unsafe. These grave events, coupled with the economic upsurge of the empire at the end of the ninth century, "led the bankers of Baghdad to modern innovations." In 941, Kurdish bandits attacked a caravan transporting sums of gold and silver worth three million dinars, carrying off all of it. Thus it was "to avoid the transportation of currency, both dangerous and cumbersome, that the bankers made constant use of letters of exchange, letters of credit, and promissory notes." These are translations of Arabic expressions about whose precise meaning there is no doubt. This system, which does not surprise us today, was born in Mesopotamia before being used in Europe. The founding of the anti-caliphate by the Fatimids in Cairo greatly changed this state of affairs. The Jewish bankers were attracted to Cairo and later to Cordova. But it is important to point out that this commercial technique began in Baghdad. The metal tablets payable on demand, used by the Assyrian merchants, had been long forgotten. Besides, they were not at all the same type of thing.

The city had suffered two sieges, under Amin and under Musta'in, and a series of street battles which spared neither men nor buildings. There were also natural disasters, floods, fires, and famines—which often took on disturbing proportions. These catastrophes recurred regularly.

The floods of the Tigris (there were at least a dozen between 883 and 945) caused considerable damage, especially in what remained of the Round City in the vicinity of the Kufa Gate. Buildings collapsed, burying many inhabitants in the rubble. Rents went up at an unforeseen rate; repairs were not made. The baths, the little neighborhood mosques, and even the markets were deserted. When gangs of pillagers invaded the main streets, horns were sounded to warn the inhabitants of Baghdad that they were coming.

Fires were frequent between 850 and 950, and they often involved entire sections of the city. They were usually caused by riots, and it was mainly the Karkh neighborhood that was damaged. Three fires in particular should be mentioned, the first one because it shows the concern of the public authorities, the second because of the frightful extent of the damage, and the third because it was accompanied by looting, which will be discussed more extensively in sections on the centuries which followed. During the reign of Wathiq, who died in 847, a fire broke out in the market places. Large sums of money were distributed among those who had been burned out so that they could rebuild their shops with plaster and brick and have iron doors installed. As a result, they were better off than before. In 935, a fire raged through the perfumers', the druggists', the silk merchants', and the jewelers' *suqs*. The result was so serious an economic crisis that the area could not be immediately rebuilt. Then, in 944, a great fire in Karkh swept from the Arch of the Belt Merchants to the fishmongers and reached the paper merchants and the sandal dealers. The storekeepers did their best to save their merchandise, but they were robbed by looters.

The last hundred years of the Abbasid caliphate were marked by urban destruction, but there was also a great deal of construction of public buildings. The hospital built by Harun al-Rashid must have been forgotten; the chronicles do not even tell us where it was situated. But the vizier Ali ibn Isa had a hospital built in the northern section of Harbiya. In the instructions to the famous physician Sinan ibn Thabit, we learn that special measures were taken concerning prisoners in times of epidemics. In 918, another hospital, founded by Muqtadir's mother, was established on the southern edge of the Shammasiya section. The caliph himself had another hospital built on the Khuld Palace square. The Buyid prince Adud al-daula had this hospital enlarged.

The increase in the number of hospitals during Muqtadir's reign caused the authorities to give a great deal of consideration to the problem of medical competence. The chief physician of one of these hospitals, Sinan ibn Thabit, reorganized the teaching of medicine, and diplomas were earned with great difficulty.

The description by the traveler Ibn Hauqal, who lived in Baghdad toward the end of the first half of the tenth century, is most appropriate at this point.

"The caliph's palace and park extended for two parasangs and were protected by a single wall. Beyond the caliph's palace, buildings lined the Tigris and went up as far as Shammasiya for about five miles, facing on the west bank the Harbiya section; then the built-up area extended down along the Tigris to Karkh. The east bank was called the Bab al-Taq or the Rusafa section.

"The west bank took the name of Karkh. On four sites in this neighborhood were mosques where public prayer took place on Friday; one of them is siutated in the very city of Abu Ja'far; another, in Rusafa, serves the inhabitants of

Bab al-Taq; another, in the caliph's palace, serves as a cathedral mosque for the aristocracy and the people; the Baratha mosque is also located on the west bank and was founded by the emir of the faithful, Ali. The buildings continue along the west bank, opposite the caliph's residence, to Kalwadha, a medium-sized city provided with a cathedral mosque which can be considered as part of Baghdad, since many inhabitants of the capital go there to pray.

"The two banks are today joined by a bridge at the end of Bab al-Taq. There were two of them at one time, but because of the small number of people who cross over, one of them, needing repairs, has been closed to traffic. Most of the neighborhoods have fallen into decay. Formerly, buildings extended from the Khurasan Gate to the bridge and then on to Bab Yasiriya, on the west bank. One notices that an area of about five miles in width has been abandoned and the buildings have been destroyed. The liveliest section today is the Karkh bank, because the people of Yasiriya go there and most of the commercial houses are found there. The trees and the canals of the east bank and the caliph's residence are fed by the waters of the Nahrawan and the Tamarra; they took from the Tigris only a small quantity of water, which would not have been enough for cultivation. The west bank took its water from the Nahr Isa, which branched from the Euphrates near Anbar under the Dimimma Bridge and was the source of small canals. These joined to form a stream called the Sarat, which also flowed in the direction of Baghdad. On its banks were many cultivated fields which made up part of the west bank of the city. It was the source of many canals which watered the crops of the region and through which flowed the excess water of the Little and the Big Sarat before it emptied into the Nahr Isa in the middle of Baghdad. On its banks stood private homes, mansions, and orchards. The Nahr Isa is navigable from the Euphrates to its junction with the Tigris, but on the Sarat are dams and obstacles which prevent navigation, dikes, and irrigation wheels. Ships come up to the bridge; their cargo is unloaded and transferred to other ships on the other side of the dam."

5.

THE GOLDEN AGE OF ARAB AND ISLAMIC CULTURE

"BAGHDAD, AT THE CONFLUENCE OF TWO CULTURES, Aramaean and Greek, became, in the tenth century, the intellectual center of the world." As capital of the caliphate, Baghdad was also to become the cultural capital of the Islamic world.

Our purpose is to show, as briefly as possible, the role that this region played in the transmission of the knowledge of antiquity, in the evolution of religious attitudes, and in the flowering of Arabic literature. We shall not try to find out, any more than did the caliphs of the period, whether the actors were Iranians, Arabs, Moslems, Christians, or Jews. Men of letters and of science had gathered in this city either through cultural affinity or because they had been summoned to the caliph's court for their worth or their competence.

An effort was made to keep the language and the religion at an indispensable cultural level. In reality, there was but a single aim: It was necessary to study the structure and the rules of the language of the Koran in order to have the language respected and understood. We shall not spend too much time on the grammatical work, since we want to follow the more universal tendencies, especially in their influence on medieval Europe. We shall mention only Khalil, the inventor of Arabic prosody, the first author of a dictionary, and especially his pupil Sibawaih, who has the distinction of having codified definitively all the problems of grammar. Later, Mubarrad wrote a work which is not only didactic but a valuable collection of poetic quotations. He also shares with his rival and contemporary, Tha'lab, the honor of having contributed to the philological training of several poets.

Some authors wrote the biography of Mohammed in the broad sense, by including the literature of the *hadith*, "The Conversations of the Prophet." The names of two of the first authors in this category should be remembered: Muhammad ibn Ishaq and Ibn Hisham.

Two of the founders of the four schools of jurisprudence lived in Baghdad and exerted decisive influence there for a long time. Abu Hanifa is already known to us because of his material participation in the founding of the city. He had the merit of integrating into the formalism of the law a living element, which consisted of both an analogical method and, when necessary, personal common sense. His tomb is still venerated in Baghdad. Opposed to this type of thought stands Ibn Hanbal, whose followers were talked about a great deal during the early centuries of the Mesopotamian city. This austere traditionalist was perhaps the victim of his own work, which is nothing more than a collection of *hadith*. Indeed, he came to consider tradition, after the Koran, as the only source of law. A fierce enemy of all innovation, Ibn Hanbal created a puritan school within Islam, which still in our day inspires the people of the Saudi kingdom. His tomb was in Baghdad too, but it has disappeared.

The first commentaries on the Koran were written in Baghdad but we shall not spend much time on them. Religious circles were affected by a contemplative movement begun by the Mutazilites, etymologically "those who keep to themselves," as they did during the political quarrels which divided the Moslems the century before. The Mutazilites, preaching essentially that God was a Perfect Being, took no attributes other than his unity into account. This conviction led the believers to deny the eternity of God's word; thus, for them, the text of the Koran became a creation of the Divinity. This doctrine, with its appeal to reason, is particularly important because three caliphs imposed it officially upon the people in a particularly unpleasant way.

The religious spirit, moreover, was to be undermined by Jahiz and, even more violently, by Razi. It was during this time that the doctor of laws, Ash'ari, sprang up from the Mutazilite ranks. He dominated and definitively unified all the future beliefs of Islam. He is mentioned now because he lived during this period, but his influence will be seen in the discussion of the Seljuk period when his ideas had official approval.

During the two hundred years after A.D. 750, the intellectual ferment did not lessen for a single moment. Even limited to the names of those scholars, writers, and poets who absolutely should be known, the list is an impressive one.

Even before the founding of Baghdad, whose well-earned fame grew for at least four centuries, the caliph Mansur sullied his own reputation by having Ibn Muqaffa', the creator of secular Arabic prose, put to death for what were probably political reasons. The writer was only thirty-six years old when he was executed in 757. The caliph thus did away with the reputed translator of the *Fables of Bidpai*, known today under the title of *Kalila and Dimna*. It is a masterpiece of Arabic prose, whose literary qualities have never been denied by Arab writers.

Mamun was the caliph who was largely responsible for cultural expansion. An Arab historian states the following:

"He looked for knowledge where it was evident, and thanks to the breadth of his conceptions and the power of his intelligence, he drew it from places where it was hidden. He entered into relations with the emperors of Byzantium, gave them rich gifts, and asked them to give him books of philosophy which they had in their possession. These emperors sent him those works of Plato, Aristotle, Hippocrates, Galen, Euclid, and Ptolemy which they had. Mamun then chose the most experienced translators and commissioned them to translate these works to the best of their ability. After the translating was done as perfectly as possible, the caliph urged his subjects to read the translations and encouraged them to study them. Consequently, the scientific movement became stronger under this prince's reign. Scholars held high rank, and the caliph surrounded himself with learned men, legal experts, traditionalists, rationalist theologians, lexicographers, annalists, metricians, and genealogists. He then ordered instruments to be manufactured."

Astronomical observation was begun in Baghdad in an observatory in the Shammasiya section, on the left bank of the Tigris, east of Rusafa. The staff set to work measuring the ecliptic angle and fixing the position of the stars. In addition, the caliph ordered that two terrestrial degrees be calculated in order to determine the length of the solar year. (This work was not to be taken up again for seven centuries.) The engineer Ibrahim Fazari, who helped plan the founding of Baghdad, was the first in the Arab world to make astrolabes. (The Bibliothèque Nationale in Paris has perhaps the oldest instrument of this type, one dating from the year 905. It was probably made in Baghdad, since it has on it the name of an heir apparent to the caliphate, a son of the caliph Muktafi.)

People of the West should publicly express their gratitude

to the scholars of the Abbasid period, who were known and appreciated in Europe during the Middle Ages. There were the astronomer al-Khwarizmi (850), from whose name comes the word "algorithm"; Farghani, whom we call Alfraganus (about 850); the physician Yahya ibn Masawayh, called Mesua in the West; the astronomer Abu Ma'shar, the Albumasar of the Europeans (about 996).

The caliph Mamun was responsible for the translation of Greek works into Arabic. He founded in Baghdad the Academy of Wisdom, which took over from the Persian university of Jundaisapur and soon became an active scientific center. The Academy's large library was enriched by the translations that had been undertaken. Scholars of all races and religions were invited to work there. They were concerned with preserving a universal heritage, which was not specifically Moslem and was Arabic only in language. The sovereign had the best qualified specialists of the time come to the capital from all parts of his empire. There was no lack of talented men. The rush toward Baghdad was as impressive as the horsemen's sweep through entire lands during the Arab conquest. The intellectuals of Baghdad eagerly set to work to discover the thoughts of antiquity.

Harun al-Rashid, Mamun's father, was particularly interested in the physicians brought to his capital. The physicians who had become justly famous under the first caliphs of Baghdad had been students at the Persian school of Jundaisapur. The first representative of the famous Bakhtyashu family came from this school, too. The family furnished physicians to the Abbasid court for more than 250 years. The biography of one of them indicates that the examination of urine was a common practice.

The Nestorian Christian, Yahya ibn Masawayh, wrote many works on fevers, hygiene, and dietetics. His was the first treatise on ophthalmology, but he was soon surpassed in this field by his famous pupil, Hunain ibn Ishaq. Their books are of special value since there is no Greek treatise on the subject.

Particular mention should be made of the man to whom Arab science owes so much, the man who could be called the father of Arab medicine, Hunain ibn Ishaq, also a Christian. In medieval Latin translations he was known as Johannitius. For him the caliph Mutawakkil restored the translation bureau, which had been originally established by Mamun. Not only did Hunain work at translations, but he directed a team of scholars. His enthusiasm was responsible for great progress. He can be credited with having greatly increased the scientific knowledge of the Arabs. By inventing medical and philosophical terms, he was largely instrumental in forming a scientific language. Thanks to him and his collaborators, Arab writers formed the cultural avant-garde for a century or two. In the field of morals, this school was the first to translate the Hippocratic Oath.

Razi, the physician of genius known in medieval Europe as Rhazes, profited greatly from these works. His own medical work was extensive. This fine clinician, who had universal interests, had his differences with the Moslem religion because he was opposed to all dogmatism. For this reason, extremely violent diatribes were directed against him.

The way in which the caliph Mamun kindled the enthusiasm of others is admirable. Three brothers, the sons of Musa ibn Shakir, sought to distinguish themselves by giving fabulous sums of money to collect manuscripts and to bring translators together. The Banu Musa were themselves scholars who made advances in mathematics and astronomy.

Kindi, who was to be known to posterity by the honorary title "philosopher of the Arabs," lived in Baghdad in this richly intellectual milieu. Because of his Mutazilite convictions, he attained the threefold position of translator, teacher, and astrologer. With him, "Arab intelligence rises to the level of philosophy." Of the role he played, it is enough to say that he was the creator of a doctrine that was to flourish in Arab philosophy, the idea of conciliation between the positions of Aristotle and Plato.

Kindi's successor, Farabi, who lived in later years at the court of the Hamdanid princes in Aleppo, had his early training in Baghdad. Without detracting from Kindi's merit, a pre-eminent place must be given to Farabi, who, with his more scientific mind, was the true creator of Arab peripateticism. This "second master," after Aristotle, continued along Kindi's path, too, in affirming the similarity of Aristotle's and Plato's views. In addition, he adopted the platonic theory of emanation. His *Model City* is an adaptation from Greek philosophy in which he describes his conception of the perfect city. This scholar, who was also an excellent music theorist, contributed to the evolution of philosophical language. This master of logic also created a harmonious system that was a credit to his merit, his rigor, and his knowledge.

In the meantime, the paper industry was born. After the battle of Talas in the Ili Valley at the end of the Umayyad period, a Chinese prisoner of war had been brought to Samarkand. There he began a paper industry using linen and hemp, imitating what he had seen in his own country. In 795, mention is made of the creation of the first paper factory in Baghdad. For a long time Samarkand remained the center of the industry, but, in addition to Baghdad, paper was manufactured in Damascus, Tiberias, Tripoli in Syria, Yemen, the Maghreb, and Egypt. The city of Jativa in Spain was famous for its thick, glazed paper.

After the appearance of paper, the number of manuscripts multiplied from one end of the Moslem empire to the other. This prosperous period for the publishing and selling of books was essential for cultural development. Paper was, therefore, of prime importance in the ninth century. From then on the book business was established in the Orient. However, we do not know whether the publishing was done by the author, a specialized merchant, or both at the same time. Well-stocked bookshops were often set up around the main mosque. Scholars and writers met in them, and copyists were hired there. In addition to the public libraries open to everyone, Jean Sauvaget, quoting an Arab source, spoke of "reading rooms where anyone, after paying a fee, could consult the work of his choice."

Readers squabbled over works copied by well-known calligraphers, whose names were scrupulously recorded in the chronicles. The main libraries had their official copyists and their appointed binders. Wealthy writers had teams of such people.

As is well known from monuments and manuscripts, calligraphy was an important art in Moslem countries. The most famous of the calligraphers of the time was Ibn Muqla, who was unfortunate enough to have been the vizier of three caliphs, an honor that earned him the cruel punishment of having his right hand amputated. It is said that he attached a reed pen to his arm and wrote so well that there was no difference between the way he wrote before and after he lost his hand.

Baghdad had become an intellectual metropolis, an achievement which was to overshadow the efforts made by its two rival cities, Kufa and Basra. The work of the enthusiastic translators was only the beginning; there was a very intimate rapport between the Arab writers and Greek thought, and the attempted assimilation was often quite successful.

A little later, there also developed in Baghdad the famous quarrel between the partisans of culture stemming from the text of the Koran and the pre-Islam poets and their adversaries, the writers of Persian origin who controlled the administration of the caliphate. The writers' leader, Sahl ibn Harun, was director of the Academy of Wisdom, which played a considerable role in literature. The discussions, which were very violent at times, were favorable to the development of Arab literature. The "Arab" party, if it can be called that, defended itself stubbornly and glorified as well as it could its religious position which made of the Koran a revelation in the Arabic language. It also exalted its ancient poems, which were not really under attack. Both sides carried on the entire campaign in Arabic. Thus adversaries and partisans of Arab intellectual life agreed in honoring Arabic.

In two of his letters, Ibn Muqaffa' freely used the Arabic word *adab*, a term which needs some explanation since it covers a wide variety of ideas, such as to conform to the dictates of a strict religious spirit, to adhere to the customs of polite society. The term is somewhat similar to the ancient *arete*, with the omission of military courage. There are the same elements of practical morals, the feeling for justice, strength of soul, and piety. Good manners and courtesy became almost a technique and were, together with pure morality, the basis of Moslem education. But under the influence of the desire for cultural attainment, the term acquired a figurative sense which necessarily included the knowledge of Arab philosophy, of poetry and ancient stories, and of stylistic elegance.

Under the Abbasids, there was also the social advancement of administrative secretaries, which enabled them to succeed the poets of an earlier period, who had been the only ones to earn their living in the field of letters. Thereafter the scholars, mathematicians, astronomers, astrologers, and translators of the works of Greek antiquity were supported by the first caliphs of Baghdad.

The political history of this period is rather bleak. If only the succession of events were to be taken into consideration, we would have a false view of the cultural civilization under the Abbasids.

Moreover, the Iranization of the empire had an influence on the way of thinking, feeling, and writing. The discovery of Sassanian antiquity and Hellenic thought at the same time added fresh impetus. In the field of literature, there was a somewhat co-ordinated Iranophile movement called *shu-'ubiya*. It consisted of a reaction, not always calm or tender, against Arab domination, both political and cultural. The promoter of this anti-Arab opposition was Sahl ibn Harun, director of the Academy of Wisdom, but in all fairness it should be said that even before him there were members of the fabulous Barmekid family who were prominent during Harun al-Rashid's reign because of their omnipotence and their tragic fate. They realized that poets played the same role as modern journalists. Poets should not, therefore, be led to oppose the regime. These great ministers were also famous for their broad tolerance; that the underlying motive was either coolness toward Islam or faithfulness to Iranian beliefs does not alter the facts. We know, for example, that a number of famous disputants among Islamic theologians, free-thinkers, and doctors of different sects met at the home of the educated and enlightened Yahya, the grandson of Barmek.

Thus, in ninth-century Baghdad a fertile literary center

was formed which lighted the way for Arab letters. Poetry continued to be cultivated with the same care. The poets of the Abbasid period were worthy of their great ancestors of pre-Islamic times and of the Umayyad court. A list of the poets of genius would include: Bashshar ibn Burd, who died in 783, the standard-bearer of the *shuʻ ubiya* and an erotic poet of great talent and robustness whose capabilities were rather disturbing from a religious point of view; Mutiʻ ibn Iyas, who died in 787, as famous for his debauchery as for his blasphemy, as skillful in praising as in attacking; Saiyid Himyari, who died in 789, a more or less sincere panegyrist, who sought protection in the traditional way, who is particularly praised by the critics for his simplicity of style, and, as far as we are concerned, who escaped banality by his Shiʻite convictions, by the variety of his poetic themes, and by his artistic qualities; Abbas ibn Ahnaf, who died in 808, who speaks of the "power of love," always expressed his thoughts delicately and thus stands in opposition to the licentious poets who surrounded him, which explains his success in Spain; Abu Nuwas, who died in 813, the singer of the joy of living, the greatest Bacchic poet in the Arabic language, a sensual, debauched devil who became a hermit toward the end of his life and left a number of religious poems.

Mutiʻ ibn Iyas and Abu Nuwas, two great lyric poets, had a pronounced taste for scandal and blasphemy. It would be an exaggeration to claim that they represented fairly accurately a certain aspect of Baghdad society. Yet, the smutty tales of the *Book of Songs* prove that the upper bourgeoisie was hardly overcome with moral scruples. Drunkenness was common, it seems, and perhaps even more violent thrills were sought. These poems, however, should be taken into account as a reflection of a part of society which was hungry for pleasure.

Our honors list also includes Muslim ibn Walid, who died in 823, author of love poems and drinking songs; Abu Tammam (843) and Buhturi (897), famous for their original odes and their anthologies of poetry; Di'bil (960), who lived in peril because he associated with robbers and wrote satires in truculent and unpolished language; Ibn Rumi (896), whose verses include philosophical ideas and a close look at reality and whose satires are fine and cruel without being vulgar; Ibn Mu'tazz (908), who was caliph for one day and paid for it with his life, who, as a poet of transition, painted the society around him, describing the caliph's palaces in a rather delicate style, and who, in a moving poem, gave a glimpse of the future decadence of the caliphate; Ibn Dawud (910), leader of the school of courtly love and early ancestor of our troubadours; and, above all, the peerless Abul-Atahiya (825), the earliest Arab philosopher-poet, who wrote of suffering in verses that proclaim the vanity of the joys of this world.

The anthologies of these poets were compiled perhaps to combat the Iranian spirit of the *shu'ubiya* in an attempt to conserve the masterpieces of the pre-Islamic period.

Songs and music are perhaps more important in Baghdad than in other regions of the Moslem world. There are great names in the field of theory, Farabi for example, and in composition, the Mausilis, father and son, and Ibrahim ibn Mahdi, the ephemeral caliph. During the reigns of several Abbasid caliphs, the Mausilis delighted the court of Baghdad. Ibrahim (804) had been the favorite of the caliphs Mahdi, Hadi, and Harun al-Rashid; he was the hero of some rather racy adventures. He led his musicians with a baton and was perhaps the first orchestra conductor. The great historian Ibn Khaldun wrote, "The beautiful concerts given at Baghdad have left memories that still last."

Several poets gave accounts of the lives of the gay blades and the tough characters who frequented the cabarets of the capital. One small work, by Washsha, contains a sketch of the worldly manners and customs of the refined class of Baghdad and is a veritable manual of the life of the dandies of the period. It also gives minute details on dress, furniture, gold and silver utensils, cushions, and curtains, with their appropriate inscriptions.

Another writer, Azdi, who is reminiscent of Villon, describes the society of debauched party-goers. His poems are difficult to translate because of their truculence, their strong language, and their defiance of decent morals.

We should not be too surprised at the contrast between the studious world of the translator and the medical specialists and that of the writers of licentious poetry who sang, with some talent, of pleasure and debauchery and bragged of overtly displayed corruption.

The Abbasid golden age gave rise to a capable and imposing group of translators, who tried successfully to regain the heritage of antiquity. Men of letters took advantage of this substantial contribution. They entered into passionate and fruitful discussions, which were dominated by the astonishing personality of Jahiz (d.868). He is probably the greatest master of prose in all Arab literature. He was a prolific writer with a vast field of interest. In addition, his Mutazilite convictions made him a literary leader. In order to describe reality, he broke with a tradition which was bound to the past. He laid the foundations of a humanism which was almost exclusively Arab and hostile to Persian interference at the beginning, and which took on more and more Greek coloration later on. His love of knowledge and his great intellectual honesty are evident on every page of his works. Jahiz is outstanding because of his exceptional genius, his qualities of originality, and his art in handling an often cruel and sometimes disillusioned irony, in which he was more successful than any writer before him. Jahiz pushed sarcasm to the point of mocking irreverence toward Divinity, more in the style of Lucian than of Voltaire. It is due to the tremendous talent of this prodigious artist that Arabic prose became more important than poetry.

Another great writer, Ibn Qutaiba, ranks high, immediately after Jahiz, whom he survived by about twenty years (d.889). He too had an intellectually curious mind which made him a grammarian, a philologist, a lexicographer, a literary critic, a historian, and an essayist. In literature, he is an advocate of conciliation, through conviction and not lassitude, and a partisan of the golden mean. His *Book of Poetry*, which shows him to be a creator of the art of poetry, contains judgments of great value.

Ibn Duraid is worthy of mention because of the role recently attributed to him by an Arab critic as creator of the *Maqama*, of the *Seance*, which will be discussed later. This philologist is one of the last contestants in a battle which, during his lifetime, interested very few men of letters, the battle against Iranophilia.

Mas'udi must certainly not be neglected, not only because he was born in Baghdad but because this tireless traveler has left us a most interesting account of the history of the Abbasid caliphate.

The writer of memoirs, Suli, is of interest because he speaks of events of which he was a sad and, at times, indignant witness. His contemporary, Mas'udi, says, "He reports details which have escaped others and things which he alone could have known."

The date of Tanukhi's death (994) places him in the Buyid period, as does his style, but in one of his works he speaks especially of the upheaval during Muqtadir's reign. Although it was meant to entertain, this book, written in a lively style, contains a good deal of solid judgment. Another short work consists of a series of amusing, merry stories which, if taken too seriously, might give a disturbing picture of the Baghdad bourgeoisie. It is dangerous to generalize, since the book is probably about a circle of party-goers and unscrupulous revelers. In short, reading Tanukhi is quite amusing.

It is impossible to mention all the prose writers who added to the glory of the ninth century in the Arabic language. Those who spent several years in Baghdad profited from the extraordinarily feverish atmosphere of the place. We must not omit Ya'qubi, the geographer, who left us exciting pages on the founding of Baghdad, and Ibn Hauqal who used Baghdad as the point of departure for his voyages.

The object of this résumé is to show the splendor of the literary milieu of the time. Profiting from circumstances which revealed the secrets of Hellenism to them, the writers became the "keepers of Greek wisdom" and humanists of a cultural scope to be envied by future generations.

The cultured residents of Baghdad liked their pleasure. They gathered secretly in cabarets, and some of them met in Christian monasteries on the outskirts of the city. The *Book of Convents* by Shabushti is really a description of the city's taverns. Wine was certainly drunk in these places. The Bacchic poets of the time were there to testify to that. Snow sherbets were eaten. Concerts were given in rooms cooled by *punkahs*. Abu Nuwas exclaims, "In how many taverns did I land during the night cloaked in pitch-like blackness! The cabaret owner kept on serving me as I kept on drinking with a beautiful white girl close to us." Gambling houses were also popular. Chess, especially, was highly favored and backgammon was second in popularity. It is probable that the shadow-theater was a form of entertainment also.

The privileged at the caliph's court were probably invited to play polo or go hunting. Horse racing for the aristocratic public and cock-fights and ram-fights for a lower level of society were common pastimes.

Popular entertainment was offered in public places. First there were the preachers, who not only delivered homilies. Perhaps they also told stories, such as the ones which were the origin of *The Thousand and One Nights*. Mas'udi writes, "In Baghdad, there was a street storyteller who amused the crowd with all sorts of tales and funny stories. His name was Ibn Maghazili. He was very amusing and could not be seen or heard without provoking laughter. As he told his stories, he added many jokes which would have made a mourning mother laugh and would have amused a serious man." There were also street hawkers who offered extraordinary products to their gaping customers. There was even a man with diseased eyes who sold passers-by a cure for ophthalmia.

We should have liked to gather archaeological evidence about the city's past. There would have been a great deal of it; the remains of Samarra could have supplied information not very long ago. We should have liked to learn about the quality of an artistic civilization that we know only through comments in books.

Our enthusiasm is somewhat satisfied by the beautiful descriptive poems by Buhturi, but it is risky to depend upon poetry to analyze a piece of architecture or even to enjoy its decorative aspects.

We have no authentic documents from the earlier periods on the art of the city of Baghdad itself, but we do have several vague but enthusiastic descriptions by writers. They speak of porticoes and cupolas; they go on at length about the luxuriously rich furniture in the various palaces, as we have seen in the description of the Byzantine ambassador's reception. Mural paintings are especially mentioned.

At this point it is appropriate to add two quotations that contain a good deal of information. The first is from the poet Bashshar ibn Burd, who was blind. He had ordered a vase from a Basra potter and questioned the artisan about its decoration. The potter answered, "Flying birds." The poet, thinking of the pouncing animal motif which was popular at the time, said, "You should have put a predator above, ready to swoop down on them."

The great artist Abu Nuwas also clearly indicates the tastes of the time. "Wine flows among us in an ornate goblet in which the Persians had carved all sorts of figures. Horsemen, at Khosrau's side, aim at an antelope with their arrows."

Fortunately, the art of Samarra makes up in part for the gaps. This decoration on plaster is bold, marked with holes, and is elegantly winding with deep, sinuous grooves. The paintings of the palace of Samarra disappeared during World War I, and we know them only through the publication by E. Herzfeld, who brought them to light. Some have remained famous and appear in all the works dealing with Moslem frescoes. There are two women dancers who approach each other and pour wine into a goblet. The flowers and the various animals recall the classic art of the Hellenic east. But of particular interest is a solemn figure, draped in a robe decorated with a wheel motif, whose shoulders are covered with a striped hood. This could very well represent a monk. If so, it brings to mind the painting with which

Mutawakkil, the inveterate drunkard and persecutor of Shi'ites and non-Moslems, had his palace decorated. It was of an assembly of monks in a church choir and was a copy of a fresco that he had admired in a monastery in the suburbs of Baghdad.

In the third quarter of the tenth century, Mesopotamian painters were invited to Egypt to paint frescoes. The story is told by Maqrizi, who refers to a *History of Painters*, which can be placed in the eleventh century. The passage is reminiscent of Mesopotamia. The paintings of lapis lazuli, vermilion, verdigris, and other colors were covered over with varnish. We are told that the relief of these frescoes was remarkably executed in the style of the Basra painters.

Samarra sent for glassmakers and potters from Basra, and for more potters and color mixers from Kufa. A Chinese text insists that Chinese artists taught painting in Akula (the Syriac name for Kufa), in Lower Mesopotamia. The problem, which has not been solved, is an interesting one since it concerns a region which later became famous for its book decorations.

Although we do not know exactly where these industries and crafts were located in the earlier period, we know that Mesopotamia was much advanced in weaving and ceramic techniques and in brick and wood sculpture.

Fortunately, an Arabic text tells of the quality of the ceramic mural tiles that were sent from the Mesopotamian capital, along with other materials, to decorate the mihrab of the Great Mosque of Qairawan: "These precious faïence panels were imported for a reception room that the Aghlabid emir wanted to build, and also beams of teakwood from which to make lutes. He had the pulpit for the Great Mosque made of it. The mihrab was brought in the form of marble panels from Iraq. He placed the faïence tiles on the façade of the mihrab. A man from Baghdad made tiles which he added to the first ones." And, indeed, Georges Marçais, who studied this decoration carefully, wrote, "Two origins can be distinguished. One, with a more skillful and a richer design using enamel of various colors, consisted of exotic pieces; the other, of simpler, larger decorations in one color, consisted of locally manufactured pieces." We find "a very wide decoration composed of very simple geometric combinations interlaced with floral forms, as in the linear groove decoration of columns and carved wood."

Many specimens of pieces of ceramic vessels were found in the Samarra excavations. These too are of yellow and green glazed pottery.

When the Arab historians describe the famous Cupola of the Donkey, with its gently rising ramp, they speak also of the minaret with the spiral ramp in the Samarra mosque.

All the briefly mentioned documents give evidence of a great unity of style, and Baghdad can be credited with a floral decoration which, although already conventional, was not yet geometric.

Great admiration should be expressed for this civilization born in Baghdad. In this center of universal culture were found polite manners, refinement, general education, and the confrontation of religious and philosophical thought which made the Mesopotamian city the queen of the world during that period.

6.

THE BUYID PROTECTORATE

SOME OF THE OFFICERS of the soldiers of fortune founded a dynasty which became powerful enough to place the caliphate under its protection. This in itself was a new and important political occurrence, but there was something even more original about it. Until this period, the slight move toward independence, which was only occasionally successful, had taken place in the eastern part of the empire. With the new Buyid princes, the western provinces were heard from. The chief weakness of these princes was that they were as numerous as they were ambitious. They had to share as well as they could the area to be exploited, which led to fratricidal combat.

The Buyids entered the battle in 935, occupied Fars the following year, conquered Jibal in 935, and invaded Kerman in 936. Ten years later, the Buyid prince Mu'izz al-daula entered Baghdad. The settling of the Buyids in the capital of the caliphate was a tragi-comic episode. Mu'izz al-daula did not know a word of Arabic and had to use an interpreter. After he had received the titles that he sought and the right to have his name on coins, he needed to have a caliph at his disposal. Two weeks later, during a ceremonial reception at the caliph's palace, two Buyid officers presented themselves to the caliph, to whom they spoke in Persian. The caliph Mustakfi did not understand a blessed word of their harangue. He held his hand out to them thinking that they wanted to kiss it. The two officers knocked him off his throne, bound him with his turban, took him off to prison, and had his eyes put out. That was how the chief of the crude gangs carried out his *coup d'état*. The new master obviously had no more regard for the caliph's person than did his Turkish predecessors. In the meantime, the Abbasid vizier had quickly bestowed upon the Buyid prince the title of Emir of Emirs. Many considered as a bad omen the famine and the plague epidemic which broke out in the same year. Carcasses, dogs, and even children were eaten.

The most glorious reign was that of Adud al-daula (who died in 985), the only member of the whole family who governed the entire family territory, or most of it. The members of the family did not get along with each other well enough to maintain too prestigious or complicated a policy. Their profession of the Shi'ite faith did not help matters, since they held the caliph under their thumb. He was supreme pontiff of Sunnism but governed only his palace.

Just as soon as he could, the caliph sought to get out of this situation by recognizing the sovereignty of a Turkish officer, Mahmud, called the Ghaznavid because he had settled in Ghazna. He is remembered as the first conqueror of India and especially as the patron of three great men of letters, Firdausi, Avicenna, and Biruni. The caliph's move, which left no lasting effect, was justified by the fact that the new dynasty was Sunnite.

Later, Turkish officers in the service of the Ghaznavids revolted and succeeded in founding an empire which unified for a time all the Persian regions. At first, theirs was a history of brigandage and looting. They were demanding, they looted, they negotiated, and finally they soundly defeated the Ghaznavid army. One of their chiefs, Toghrulbeg, set up a government in Nishapur in 1038. The hard-pressed Buyids tried to negotiate as the Turkish hordes invaded Mesopotamia. Toghrulbeg's capital was moved to Ispahan. He went to Baghdad, where, through a plot, he was to become sultan, like the Ghaznavids before him. He entered the city in 1055.

Mu'izz al-daula's arrival had been accepted with indifference or even with favor by the good people of the Mesopotamian capital after the troubles that characterized the preceding years. The new Buyid master, Canard says, "repaired the canals and spent a great deal of money on his palace, all of which must have helped the people. He brought prosperity back for a time, and bread was inexpensive. Therefore, he was popular in Baghdad; there were few riots during his rule as emir."

But this was not enough to change euphoria into something more solid. The Buyids' religious convictions soon played an important part in everyday life. Baghdad had always been stirred by religious controversy, and its inhabitants did not hesitate to take to the streets to express their opinions bluntly and brutally. The people also learned from the constant revolts of the Turkish mercenaries that all they had to do was take over the streets in order to make the caliphs and viziers yield. This weakness on the part of the authorities led to anarchy.

The caliph no longer had enough power to act as arbitrator among the rival factions. It was too late for him to escape Buyid domination, and, in the course of a successful revolution, he could be swept away along with his "protectors."

Sunnites and Shi'ites fought each other in the streets of

Baghdad. The Shi'ites were strong and numerous in the Karkh section. Burning and looting went on without let-up. In their attempt to re-establish order, the members of the militia were brutal. It is not surprising that they too began to make demands.

Military disturbances were still frequent. Trouble developed between the Turks and the Dailamites at the time of caliph Muti's abdication in 963. It began again in 989, when there was a battle that lasted twelve days. Pitched fights between the two groups were won by the Dailamites, who were more numerous. Encounters were so frequent that people spoke of yearly battles. Finally, when the Dailamites began to weaken, the people of Baghdad forced them to emigrate to Wasit in 1017. Then the Khurdish contingents revolted, especially in 1042, because they were not paid on time.

During the same period, the masses remained rebellious and hard to control. In 905, people gathered in the Mansur Mosque to protest loudly against new taxes. Authority continued to be jeered at, and fires broke out everywhere. Harsh measures had to be taken, because the Karkh area was in upheaval. Of course, the *ayyar* were involved. They laid siege to the area and harassed the people in spite of the barricades which were hastily thrown up. This was the horrible situation during the first quarter of the eleventh century. The *ayyar* in effect ruled the streets. They were so well organized that they took over the collection of taxes from public authorities and terrorized the merchants. Their strength can be judged by the fact that they were in a position to exchange prisoners with the Turkish army. One of their chiefs was honored in a sermon, and another, named Burjumi, proudly led an imposing procession and was the real governor of the city for four years.

Despite their energy, the Buyids were not able to refine the customs and habits of the inhabitants of the capital. Their official Shi'ism simply offered more promises. George Makdisi has stated, "It would be a great error to consider these historical facts as having merely the same worth as curious stories, riots without any importance to the political and cultural life of the time. For we believe we have found one of the master keys to the understanding of the situation in Baghdad." Thus the religious battles in the streets give ample evidence of a sort of frenzy which was hard to appease.

The people of Baghdad were very soon invited to the commemoration of the death of Husain, the son of the caliph Ali, killed in the battle of Kerbala. Shi'ite zeal then took on an aggressive quality. The fact that they were grouped together and isolated in one area, where they had their own shrines and where they celebrated the ceremonies of their sect, developed in the Shi'ites an *esprit de corps* which degenerated into sectarianism at times. The Sunnites, who were not pleased with Shi'ite processions, sacked the Karkh district in 949. There were new clashes and victims in 957, and two years later more fights and fires.

The political results of these incidents were quickly felt. The authorities ordered the markets closed on the tenth day of Muharram. This provoked the Sunnites to riot. Evidently, although it had not yet become a custom, the Shi'ites continued to observe mourning, with some difficulty, by closing the markets and posting on the doors of the mosques signs containing propaganda and insults directed against the Umayyad caliph. It was time for the Buyid masters to take a firmer stand. According to several chronicles, in the year 963 Mu'izz al-daula ordered all shops to close and public lamentations to take place. Tents of coarse material were to be set up. Women with their hair hanging loose, their faces

87

blackened, and wearing torn clothes were to go through the streets of Baghdad crying out in Husain's memory. The Sunnites were not able to prevent this lugubrious ceremony because of the number of the Shi'ites and because of their support by the authorities.

From that time on, this ceremony became an established custom. In 970, the holiday of the Pond of Khumm was added, but the occasion was a happy one. Because of the tents that were set up and the display of patched curtains, the sad and solemn holiday often took on the character of a gigantic fair. At times, the government forbade the people of Karkh to celebrate such holidays because of fights between inhabitants of neighboring districts. This was done in 972, 974, 992, 999, and 1015. In 981 and 988, there were fires which lasted several days and which resulted in death and injury. In 1002 and 1007, there were disorders provoked by the *ayyar*. The reflections of Ibn Kathir on the beginning of the eleventh century deserve to be translated, not only because of the details they furnish, but also because they touch lightly on folkloric literature: "The *ayyar* gave rise to serious difficulties. They caused permanent disorder in the city; they carried off the wealth of the people and committed unbelievable misdeeds both night and day. They started many fires. They forced the merchants in the markets to give them money. It did no good for the police to chase them. They paid no attention to the interdictions of the authorities and kept on looting and murdering. They sowed terror among the women and children in all parts of the city. Before this worsening situation, the authorities called upon reserve troops who succeeded in dispersing these madmen and in getting rid of them forever. I believe that the anecdotes told about them call to mind the exploits of Ahmad al-Danaf, who may have really been one of them."

(Ahmad al-Danaf is a hero of *The Thousand and One Nights*.) In any event, the preceding remarks point out that the *ayyar* were very often in control of the streets during the Buyid period.

The most serious event occurred in 1029. A huge crowd rushed to the Karkh section, where looting and a horrible massacre took place. No one seemed able to stop the miniature revolution, in which the *ayyar* played a major role. Three years later, disturbances were so great that the Feast of the Breaking of the Fast could not be celebrated. Peace was restored with great difficulty. Thus, the battles between the Shi'ites and the Sunnites went on as fiercely as ever. The Sunnites' stronghold was around the Basra Gate. Makdisi believes that the neighborhood was "the fortress of the Hashimites, the pillar of the traditionalist Hanbalite movement." The Karkh section, which had suffered great hardships during Amin's siege, was the victim of constant looting. Disturbances occurred again and again between the years 1033 and 1037, when the *ayyar* became involved in Shi'ite demonstrations. In 1049, as a preventive measure, the authorities forbade Shi'ite processions, but the inhabitants of Karkh disregarded the order and erected barricades. The following year there was a successful attempt at conciliation, but it was only temporary. In 1052, the Shi'ites tried to assert themselves even more by shouting formulas of their rite in their places of worship and by writing praises of the caliph Ali on the walls. The *ayyar* interfered. The violence committed by the troops who were called out to put down the riots can be somewhat understood. The excited Sunnites set fire to the mausoleums of the Shi'ite saints. They did not even spare the tombs of the Buyid princes. The uprising lasted several months.

During this rather short period, there were not many floods

or economic crises. The terrible famine previously mentioned occurred in 946. Other famines followed in 981, 983, 993, 1002, 1047. In 978, 980, 983, and 1010 floods covered entire areas of the city.

In the middle of the eleventh century the Fatimid government of Egypt committed a grave error. It had followed with the greatest of attention the misunderstandings among the officers who held power in Baghdad. In 1034, members of a Fatimid mission were sent to the Abbasid capital to set up a propaganda service. About this time a Turkish leader of the mercenary troops appeared, named Basasiri, who had become famous by putting down an *ayyar* uprising. After a series of rather obscure events, he succeeded for a while, toward the end of 1058, in chasing the caliph from the capital. The Sunnites and the Shi'ites fought in the streets, set fires, and looted. There was nothing new about this. The Turkish militiamen were merciless in suppressing the disorders. Just like the rioters, they burned the markets of Karkh.

Basasiri, this time with the help of the *ayyar*, proved how despicable he was by parading the vizier, who had thwarted his ambitions, through the streets of the city in chains, thus offering a frightful spectacle to the people of Baghdad. The vizier was dressed in a robe of coarse wool and wore a high red felt bonnet; around his neck was a collar made of bits of leather. He was mounted on a donkey, and behind him rode an executioner who thrashed him as they went.

Evidently, the pitiful procession went through Karkh, where the Shi'ite population distinguished itself by throwing old shoes at the vizier and spitting in his face. In addition, Basasiri authorized the looting of the city and the massacre of part of the population. At his order, the demolition of the caliph's palace was begun, but only a few merlons were damaged. It was a real revolution, especially since the weekly sermon was pronounced in the name of the Fatimid caliph of Cairo.

Anarchy had been in the making for a long time. The death of Adud al-daula in 983 marks the beginning of the decadence of Buyid authority. Then there were endless family quarrels witnessed by the powerless caliphs, which alternated between the ridiculous and the tragic. Certainly the Abbasid could have and should have taken advantage of the situation. But tradition had been broken, and the monarch had resigned himself a long time before to his unobtrusive role. In the face of mounting difficulties he preferred to find a new protector and asked for the help of the Seljuk sultan, Toghrulbeg.

Buyid civilization deserves praise. Unfortunately, it flourished in particularly troubled times. The princes tried to carry out policies, some of them too late, which would bring them prestige. In 1044, for example, one of these lords had drums beaten at his door five times a day to announce time for prayer. The Buyid buildings have disappeared despite the fact that many public edifices were erected in the Mesopotamian city. In addition to the hospital founded by Adud al-daula, an Academy of Science is mentioned by writers. In the Shi'ite neighborhood of Karkh, the vizier Sabur established a library in 993. Among the more than ten thousand works were many autographs. Forty years later, most of the volumes had been eaten by worms, and the library itself was burned when Toghrulbeg entered Baghdad.

These figures do not seem exaggerated when we think of the variety and the importance of the works which were found in the bookshops of Baghdad around 987 according to a catalog of the period which is still in existence. In its preface, Ibn Nadim writes: "Here is the catalog of the books of all of the Arab nations and Persia existing in the Arabic language and writing, in the most varied scientific branches. Information will be found here on the authors, the times in which they lived, their genealogy, the dates of their births, the length of their lives, and the time of their deaths, the listing of their qualities and their faults. We review each discipline from its beginning to our time." It should be stressed that this is the first known bibliographical work. Seljuk autos-da-fé in the twelfth century put an end to the proliferation of books by suppressing all nonconformist literature.

Muqaddasi does not hide the fact that the city—the Round City—was rather dilapidated and that even the cathedral mosque was in a pitiful state. He points out the flourishing condition of the Karkh and Bab al-Taq sections and concludes, "I am afraid that the city will fall into the same ruined condition as Samarra as a result of the frequent disorders, the barbarity and the prevailing depravity, as well as the tyranny of government officials."

Near the bridge close to Bab al-Taq there was a hospital, founded in 983 by Adud al-daula, an establishment that soon acquired well-deserved fame. It had twenty physicians and admitted everyone without regard to wealth or place of residence. All political activity had become centered on the left bank of the Tigris, which was growing as an urban area. It was in this section of Shammasiya, the northwest corner, which the battles of 865 had ruined and almost turned into a desert, that Mu'izz al-daula had built his palace, surrounded by gardens and a hippodrome. He had used the iron gates of the Round City. No one was worried about the fate of Mansur's ancient city. Mu'izz al-daula's palace was destroyed fifty years later by another Buyid prince, who had his residence built on the site. Farther to the south, in the northern part of Mukharrim, Adud al-daula built a palace called *Dar al-mamlaka*, the Palace of the Principality. With cupolas and porticoes, it was a luxurious building, compared with the caliphate palace.

Decoration by the Buyids of the palaces inside the walls did not keep the caliphs from taking great care of their residences. Muqtadir was among the first to add new salons. At the beginning of the Buyid period, the caliph Muti' enthusiastically built a number of pavilions: the Peacock Pavilion, the Octagonal Pavilion, the Square Pavilion. If we may judge by this building activity, the Buyid princes were content with depriving the caliphs of all political power, but they were not concerned with impoverishing them.

As the result of a dream in which the Prophet Mohammed appeared to a holy woman, a small shrine in the Harbiya neighborhood, on the west bank, was repaired, enlarged, and raised to the rank of cathedral mosque with the authorization of the caliph Qahir in 993.

At this time, the names of the main sections of the city remained fairly much the same. To the north, there were Shammasiya and Harbiya, separated by the Tigris. On the right bank were Rusafa and the Bab al-Taq neighborhood near the Main Bridge. To the south and across the river, the Karkh area, with its teeming population, was extremely active.

The text of the historian Miskawaih concerning Adud al-daula's urban construction is worth citing: "In this year (979), Adud al-daula ordered the houses and streets of Bagdad to be rebuilt, as they had been damaged partly by arson, partly by demolition. They were a mere heap. He began with the public mosques, which also were in an absolutely ruinous condition, spending a vast sum upon them.

Such of the buildings as were beyond repair were demolished by his order and replaced with solid constructions, which were raised high, furnished, and decorated. He ordered the remunerations of the managers, muezzins, prayer-leaders, and Readers to be regularly paid, and allowances to be provided for the strangers and poor who took refuge in them; all this had been neglected and unthought of. Next he ordered the restoration of such suburban mosques as were in disrepair, and restored their trust funds. In these reforms he relied on trustworthy agents, supervised by the Registrar of the Alids. He then compelled the owners of plots which had suffered from fire and devastation during the riots to restore them to perfect condition, both buildings on them and appearance and decoration. Those who could not afford to do so were allowed to borrow from the Treasury, which was to be repaid when the borrower's circumstances improved; when the owner was untrustworthy or absent, a trustee was appointed who was allowed the sums which he required. Thus Bagdad was rebuilt and became as magnificent as it had ever been.

"Attention was now devoted to the houses and dwellings on both banks of the Tigris; embankments were built up, and balconies repaired after they had been in ruins. He ordered these officials and members of riverbank to do their best to restore and beautify them. Adud al-daula abolished the practice of demolishing and selling the materials, and ordered the restoration of the garden which formed the court of Abbas ibn Husain's palace, as also that of the Zahir Garden in the middle of the Eastern side of Bagdad; these works were carried out and these waste places were filled with flowers, plants, and buildings after they had been the haunts of dogs when they had been the dumping-grounds for carcasses and garbage. Plants were brought thither from Fars and elsewhere.

"In Bagdad there were numerous canals. From these there were various conduits used for watering people's gardens and providing water in the parts at a distance from the Tigris. Their channels had got silted up and their traces covered; fresh generations arose which knew not of them. The poor were compelled to drink the indigestible water of the wells, or else take the trouble to fetch the water of the Tigris from a long distance. Adud al-daula gave orders that their main channels and feeders should be cleared. Over the main channels, such as Nahr Isa, the Sarat, and the Khandaq, there had been bridges, which had fallen out of repair, been neglected, and left unheeded; in such cases sometimes no road was possible that way, in others they had been slightly repaired by the people of the region according to their means and with a view to economy and putting off the evil day; it constantly happened that cattle, women, children, or weaklings who crossed them fell down. All these were built afresh and firmly as solid structures. The case was similar with the Bridge of Bagdad. No one could cross it without risk to his life, especially if he was on horseback; it was so narrow, frail, and crowded; strong and massively built barges were now selected for it, it was broadened till it became like a wide road, and was protected with railings. It was besides put under the care of Watchers and guides."

We have mentioned Adud al-daula's hospital. It was seriously damaged by a flood in 1074, during which water came through the windows. Other floods in 1159 and 1174 damaged the building. But repairs must have been carried out rapidly, since Ibn Jubayr speaks of the hospital's activity. It was seriously damaged by the Mongol attack in 1258 and was little more than a ruin during Ibn Battuta's stay in the city.

The recent discovery of a gold medal with Adud al-daula's effigy on it permits us to know this prince's traits better than those of other Eastern monarchs. This lord, who claimed to be of noble descent, took the ancient Persian title "King of Kings." He appears on the medal in full face, with a rounded beard, and wearing a Sassanian crown. The effect is very impressive indeed.

The reproduction of the Buyid's portrait is not surprising. There are coins that have on them the faces of three caliphs, Mutawakkil, Muqtadir, and Muti'. As to the crown, Mas'udi could have seen the manuscript of a *History of the Kings of Persia*, illustrated with paintings of the sovereigns of Iran in court costumes. Further, the Ziyarid prince of Ispahan, Mardawij, had chosen to place upon his head a copy of the crown of the Sassanian Anushirwan. We know also, from a graffito, that Adud al-daula visited the ruins at Persepolis in 955. He could have examined at length some of the ancient Persian headdresses.

The cultural civilization of the Buyid period is perhaps an unexpected phenomenon, but it is incontestable as far as literature is concerned. A special place is reserved for a great Arab poet, the greatest in his century, Mutanabbi, who was the panegyrist of the Buyids. His place in Arab letters is firmly fixed. He deserves the highest praise; he imitates and surpasses the bards of antiquity. He is concise and goes directly to the essence of things. His style is finely delicate, his comparisons are superb, and he is justly praised for his rhythm and his wedding of words.

It is too bad to have to put next to this famous poet a versifier whose only claim to fame is his truculence. Ibn Hajjaj, who died in 1000, wrote in all genres that enabled him to earn a living. Knowing whom to flatter permitted him to devote himself to his calling, licentious poetry. One of the first characteristics noticed in his poetry, in which there is no lack of smut, is the number of expressions borrowed from vagrants or perhaps from the *ayyar*. Ibn Hajjaj, moreover, was not concerned with quality; he was satisfied with trivia and filth. Evidently, he belonged to a certain literary tradition. We have mentioned Abu Nuwas, but he was a man of genius. Ibn Hajjaj interests us today as a chronicler in verse of a shady society that was not bothered by scruples.

Although the *Book of Songs* was written in Aleppo, in the Hamdanid court, the content of Abul-Faraj's work deals so much with poets and musicians that it has to be read by anyone wanting to understand the circle in which the wits of Baghdad lived. He devotes time to the frivolous aspect of the Abbasid court and tells anecdotes which are often scandalous. We have already mentioned how interesting it is to thumb through Ibn Nadim's *Catalog*, which gives information on the collection of manuscripts in every field of thought found in the bookshops of the city.

We shall also mention a historian, Hamza Isfahani, a holdover from the *shu'ubiya*. Ibrahim Sabi played an important role in the Buyid court and, as a result, did not escape disfavor. In prison, he edited a history of the Buyid family in rhymed prose, the first of a series of panegyrics with which Arab literature was later to be encumbered. We finish our list of historians with Hilal Sabi, the grandson of Ibrahim, and especially Miskawaih, as good an annalist as he is a moralist.

There is also the birth of a prose art, which, although it refuses to take on the embellishment of poetry, does borrow its subjects. The writer is not only a creator, but an artist.

His talent is measured by lightness and elegance and considers form before ideas. His extensive knowledge is equalled by his intellectual honesty.

Two men of politics in the Buyid court were really masters in this manner of writing. Ibn Abbad and Ibn al-Amidils were at the same time the object of excessive praise because of the favors they could hand out and the object of bitter criticism on the part of the discontented. These two men were surrounded by all the men of letters of their time. We certainly appreciate their style less than their contemporaries did, for it has us floundering in bombast and overelegance.

There had to be at least one misanthrope in the circle. This was the role of Tauhidi, the greatest prose writer of the tenth century. The object of his work was to support the claims of the "have-nots" against the "haves" and to protest against the happy life and the love of comfort. We have here an outstanding and defiant representative of individualism, a writer of the first order, an implacable pamphleteer, viciously biting and often unjust. He gives evidence of exceptional mastery of the language and was, just like Jahiz before him, the most universal man of his time. Contrary to the current fashion, he does not surrender to research and affectedness. The expression which Tauhidi uses in describing his moral and physical misery is rare in Arab literature. He bemoans his poverty, and it is true that at times he did not have enough food.

We must not forget a genial writer who created a new genre, the *Maqama*, which Orientalists have translated as *Seances*. Hamadani, who died in 1007, was born in Hamadan, lived for a long time in Nishapur, and then became a wanderer. But he certainly belonged to the life of Mesopotamia as the protégé of the minister Ibn Abbad. The *Seances* consist of a group of sketches whose central character is a jack-of-all-trades, a true confidence man of unparalleled brazenness and diverting extravagance, a skillful scoundrel, and a player of practical jokes. Similar literary characters are Scapin and Figaro. The subjects of the sketches are varied, with a fierce humor which spares no one and the outrageous comedy of the theater of the fair. In these piquant little stories, full of malice, with their colorful scenes, the author gave full rein to his facetious temperament. The *Seances*, in our opinion, are written in difficult language; the substance surpasses the form, and they have a particular pungency, thanks to the author's implacable observation of living models.

But something even more serious and troubling occurs. About 963, there appeared an encyclopedia edited by a politically, philosophically, socially, and mystically inspired group called, in Arabic, *Ikhwan al-Safa*. In translation it is the *Faithful Friends*, or even the *Brothers of Purity*. This semi-secret society of free-thinkers treated all possible subjects in a series of letters. They were also innovators in that they touched upon unedited materials in a sort of scientific summa. The work surpassed by far the intellectual level of Moslem theologians of the time. It is a very pure and a very refined doctrine, a sort of aesthetic pantheism which has as its basis a universal harmony desired by the Creator. The encyclopedia was, moreover, the first popularized work to discuss techniques and occupations, and it arranged them in an original manner. According to the analysis made by Leon Brunschvig, the manual trades in the treatises "are classified either by the prime needs of men (this is especially the case for weaving), by the materials used (precious metals, perfumes), by the manufactured object (astronomical instruments), by the services rendered to people (such as those of street sweepers or bath owners), or because of skill in the arts (prestidigitators, sculptors, musicians)." Through certain insights the "Faithful Friends" showed that they had a high sense of human dignity. At any rate, Moslem orthodoxy, which was not taken in, repudiated the book.

To these various authors of works written with so much talent should be added the name of Mawardi. He belongs to the Buyid period by the date of his death, 1058, if not by his work. In the silence of his study, far from the noise of the street, he composed a treatise on public law, bringing it to a point of original and coherent perfection, which fixed the laws of political Sunnism. It is a methodical and learned treatise, the statement of a keen mind well aware of administrative problems.

Buyid art has left remarkable works. Two extraordinary examples will be mentioned because their state of preservation permits the display of their stunning decoration.

The first is a gold ewer, which is now at the Freer Gallery of Art in Washington, D.C. It bears the name of the son and successor in Baghdad of Mu'izz al-daula, Prince Bakhtiyar, who died in 978. Its splendid decoration consists of an interlaced design and animals in circles.

The second, another gold ewer now at the Cleveland Museum, was dedicated to the next to the last prince of the family, Abu Kalijar, who died in 1048. Not only does it have the name of the dedicatee, but it contains a poem by Ibrahim Sabi, whose verses evoke in terrible fashion the last gasps before the fall of the dynasty. The poem advocates the execution of the regime's adversaries in the place of animals on the Day of Sacrifices. "With your sword, cut off the heads of the Buyids' enemies and pile up victims." Interlacing ribbons unroll on the neck and on the body. Medallions are formed, in the center of which ducks and guinea fowl face each other two by two.

Artistic cloth-making was just as important as in the preceding period. Eager to have luxurious materials manufactured in their capital, the caliphs brought teams of weavers from Tuster, in Susiana. The Mesopotamian city soon had a good many workshops in which there was a growing output of superb silk and brocaded materials. The ciclatouns of Baghdad were famous.

The word "baldachin," which entered the European languages through Italian, was the name of a material before it was used for a dais. It comes from the word "Baghdad." Marco Polo used the form "Baudac," and other travelers said "Baldach." This is proof of the popularity in the Middle Ages of materials brocaded with gold and often decorated with figures, suggesting cloth manufactured in Baghdad itself.

We should mention, too, cloth called *attabi*, made of silk and cotton in various colors and greatly appreciated by Ibn Jubayr. It took its name from a section of the city, Attabiya.

There was a truly royal collection of cloths which must be attributed to the Buyid period, since one piece of the priceless series bears the date 998. These cloths were found on the site of Raiy, near modern Tehran, but they are homogeneous in style, and the Buyids, who were the real rulers from Mesopotamia to the center of Iran, could very well have ordered them from the factories of Baghdad, the center of their political activity.

This cloth has on it the figures of animals, and is thus similar to the material mentioned in the description of the Byzantine ambassador. There are variously arranged designs familiar to us today: separated circles, touching circles, circles joined and twisted together by a smaller loop, diamond shapes, and squares. There is a prodigious variety of animals. Among the birds are eagles, falcons, ducks, and particularly majestic geese. Among the quadrupeds are goats, ibexes, camels, hares, and lions. In addition, there are monsters dear to this phantasmagoric art: double-headed eagles, griffons, and sphinxes. There is a circle of ibexes bounding straight ahead in various positions. They seem to be having a lively time, and, free from all restraint, gallop gracefully in a never ending procession. This pastoral work is gay, alive, and full of verve. Yet the Kufic inscription accompanying the scene is disconcerting: "Death is a door through which everyone must pass."

There is also the figure of a person seated on a throne, as though in a kind of parade. He has his arms extended in what appears to be a praying gesture, but in reality he has a falcon in each hand.

We rarely have at our disposal masterpieces of such undeniable artistic quality. They can be considered the testimony of an era. We are struck by the extremely distinguished character of this collection, its refined elegance, and its fine execution in a series of very soft tones. The science of design is wedded to perfect technical ability. Since the inscriptions do not mention any name that has come down to us through history, we may rightly assume that we do not even have the most beautiful pieces from the workshop that manufactured them.

To this considerable lot of large and well-preserved pieces, we should add a magnificent silk cloth made into a jacket, with a proud inscription on it of strong, rigid, beautiful, and simple Kufic characters spelling out the names of Baha al-daula, the son of Adud al-daula, whose power in Mesopotamia lasted from 989 to 1012. Another piece of cloth bears the name of the last Buyid, Malik Rahim Abu Nasr, who was the master of Baghdad beginning in the year 1048.

7.

THE RISE OF THE SELJUKS

WE HAVE SEEN A SERIES of seditions and uprisings, stirred up by the regular troops and the militia and accompanied by looting and burning, pitched battles between Sunnites and Shi'ites, and recurrent economic crises followed by terrible famines. Chaos could have been the result, but the new power born in the eastern part of the empire was destined to save at least Sunnism. Toghrulbeg, who had come to Baghdad in 1055 to replace Buyid authority which had fallen to the distaff side, came to the caliph's aid in 1060. When he entered the city, he uttered sinister threats, which were later carried out. Doubtless, the caliph had sought support in his effort to free himself from insolent masters who, even worse, were Shi'ites, but he had not called for the Seljuk in order to have him set up a new despotism. In other words, the caliph and the sultan had not agreed upon an identical program. According to Claude Cahen, the caliph could choose only between oppressors and protectors. As a result, he was resigned to being a puppet.

It is difficult to analyze Toghrulbeg's feelings at the moment when he answered the appeal of the caliph, who, without loyal troops, could hardly act alone. Toghrulbeg's personal views and the prestige of holding Baghdad were enough to determine his conduct. The Buyids had shown boorish insolence in their dealings with the caliphs; the Seljuk was more formal, but even though he did not consider his victory a Sunnite triumph, he was determined to hold the caliphate in an unyielding grip. For years, Toghrulbeg had been involved in the tumultuous affairs of Baghdad. Although he now decided not to tolerate any disorder, he was not always successful. After several years, the Seljuks succeeded in governing independently vast territories which extended from Syria to Iraq, and they definitively installed Islam in Asia Minor. We feel even today all the seriousness of the breaking up of the Abbasid caliphate's domain. From this debris were born the particularist principalities, dangerous to the political and religious unity of the Moslem world. Certainly the wonderful days of the caliphate were never to return, but the new masters were to be complimented for having infused fresh blood into Islam and having made a cult of will and organization.

The Seljuks not only had very specific political ambitions, they also made many physical improvements in Baghdad, although they did not settle in the city themselves. The Round City had lost its importance a long time before, while the east bank continued to develop. The ramparts of the city of Mansur had fallen into ruins, and little by little houses began to be built on their site.

Three great sultans succeeded each other—Toghrulbeg, Alp-Arslan, and Malik-Shah, who died in 1092. Then the family broke up, and the little dynasties continued to have some relations, devoid of all amenities, with the caliphate, which tried to regain some of its power. At first the caliphs were impatient with Turkish meddling. Even if we cannot go so far as to talk of a struggle between the "priesthood and the empire," it must be admitted that there was a confrontation of basic legal opinions, although the problem had already been raised not long before by the introduction of "palace mayors." Basically, the caliph could not govern without the Seljuk strength, and the sultans got their power from the authority of the caliphs. This was not much change as far as the caliph was concerned; he had not wielded authority alone for a long time. But the Seljuks were not merely the essential element of a political revolution; they treated the caliphs with a certain amount of disdain.

Louis Massignon remarks, "At the time when the scission between spiritual power and temporal power caused the troops to be moved west to the traditional field of action, there was a growth of the palaces of temporal power, *saltana*, under the Buyid and Seljuk dynasties, and, to the west of the bridges in the center of the city, there was a symmetrical growth of the palaces of the spiritual sovereign, the caliph."

The Seljuk sultans went to Baghdad only for visits. They felt much too powerful to have to live in a city where the caliph was so subservient. They thought it sufficient to keep a High Commissioner there. A new factor arose, but, considering its failure, there is no sense in forming hypotheses on what might have been the caliph's immediate future outside of Baghdad. During the Sultan Malik-Shah's visit in 1092, he ordered the caliph to turn the city over to him and to go live anywhere else that he chose. After much equivocation, the sultan granted the caliph a delay of ten days before having to obey his order. Fortunately for the caliph, Malik-Shah died several days later.

We have seen up to this point the taking over of an almost nonexistent caliphate by a powerful sultanate. From the end of the eleventh century on, we shall see little by little the timid daring of the caliphate. This is really an illusion, since there was soon no real power to thwart its desire for autonomy. In any event, the discord among the various Seljuk princes was favorable to the resumption of power by the caliphs, at least in Baghdad and its suburbs.

From the time of the Seljuks, the fate of several religious movements was determined in the Abbasid capital. New reactions succeeded triumphant Shi'ism, triumphant at least where the imams were concerned. These reactions developed in a contrary sense with Hanbalism, which entered into battle against the newly organized Sunnism, taught in schools recently founded with the surge of Ash'arism. Karkh maintained its agitated and sometimes bloody role as citadel of the Shi'ites and continued its hostility toward its Sunnite neighbors in the Basra Gate neighborhood.

The eminently puritan doctrine of Hanbalism flourished especially during the eleventh century, despite the fact that its followers ran a certain amount of risk in preaching its ideas. They were the victims and, at times, the instigators of difficulties that kept the streets of the capital in a troubled state. The founder, Ahmad ibn Hanbal, had been born in Baghdad, he had been persecuted by state-supported Mutazilism, and he had been buried in the city. Actually, the struggle of the Hanbalites against what could be called bad morals won the support of the good Moslems. The attitude of the Hanbalites toward prostitution and intoxicating beverages could not possibly be condemned by right-minded people.

We shall now review the disasters which the various sections of Baghdad suffered during this second half of the eleventh century, whether they were caused by fights between different groups of the population or by acts of nature.

In 1057, there was a frightful famine in Baghdad. Children and even corpses were eaten. As might be expected, this disaster was followed by an epidemic of the plague.

The same year, a fire destroyed a large part of the markets on the left bank, from the Barley Gate to Muhawwal to the west. Two years later, another and even worse disaster damaged several districts, especially Karkh. The famous library founded by the Buyid vizier, Sabur ibn Ardashir, was destroyed by fire. The books which were saved were looted by the people and, of course, by the inevitable *ayyar*. The material damage was soon repaired, but another fire, the result of a fight between Sunnites and Shi'ites, broke out in the same region in 1077.

The flood of 1062 had its effect on the region of the caliph's palaces and damaged the wall of the southern part of the fortress, beginning at the gardens along the Tigris. In 1066, a fire destroyed about one hundred shops in the Mu'alla Canal neighborhood, in the southern part of the caliph's stronghold. The year before, there had been a battle between Shi'ites and Sunnites in Karkh, followed by serious fires. There were disorders in 1066, caused by Turkish troops, who looted private homes.

Between 1069 and 1075, the city underwent several damaging floods. The most serious was in 1074, which for a long time was called "the year of the flood."

The water, more than thirty feet deep, covered a considerable area. On the west bank the Harbiya cemetery was under water. The situation on the east bank was truly catastrophic. Not only were the northern cemeteries and Rusafa flooded, but the water reached the caliph's palaces up to the Pleiad Palace, at the southeast end of the stronghold. The current was so swift that it swept away all the dikes set up between the districts of the city. There was no way to count all the houses and the stores that were demolished. The disaster had been brought about by a tornado followed by torrential rains. A great deal of damage was done to the Grand Palace of the caliphs. The panic-stricken people sought refuge on higher ground, such as that near the Bab al-Taq, or on the right bank, which was less flooded. All sorts of debris and furniture were carried off by the water. For two weeks the caliph presided over public prayer on Fridays from a boat, since the water in the caliphs' mosque was as high as a man. In short, the east bank of Baghdad was in ruins for several years.

In 1075, trouble broke out for religious reasons between the inhabitants of the neighborhood around the new Nizamiya school and those of the Tuesday Market. Then the Hanbalites carried out a punitive raid against the cabarets and the prostitutes, who were banished from Baghdad. Even the pigeon-shooting fields were not spared.

The disorders of 1077 lasted five months. The entire population was involved, and was divided into two camps. Among them were civil and religious officials, the most famous of whom were the mystic Qushairi and the teacher Shirazi. Before the two groups came to blows, they argued Ash'arism and Hanbalism with a great deal of emotion. The caliph's troops were mobilized to intervene if the clashes became too violent. But it was especially during the following year that this sort of scandal became flagrant. Ten people died during a fight, and the widows of the victims gathered near the Bab al-Nubi, at the stronghold of the caliph's palaces, to ask for justice. The fight was caused by students of the Nizamiya school who had demonstrated against the Hanbalites.

The trouble of 1088 shows how excitable the people of Baghdad had become. The inhabitants of the Basra Gate neighborhood were celebrating the beginning of the construction of a new stone bridge across a canal. Masons were carrying bricks on gold and silver trays, and other persons were beating drums. People of other sections of the city joined the procession, and, as a result, the crowd became very dense. Because of a minor incident with a woman who was selling drinks, a pitched battle soon developed between the police and the people, several of whom were killed or wounded.

The *ayyar* continued to be active in such disorders. They were part of the most tumultuous groups. They helped aggravate and prolong the trouble. They were on the lookout for new movements, and, at the end of the Seljuk period, they joined the Batinites, whose furious attacks panicked the ruling classes. Terror was spread everywhere by these assassins; it is by the term assassin that these frenzied fanatics came to be known in the West in later years because of the approximate transcription of *Hashshashin* (users of hashish). They were responsible for the death of the great statesman Nizam al-mulk. No one was safe. In addition to these excesses, there were denunciations that threatened the lives of individuals. In reality, the *ayyar* sold themselves to the highest bidder. They were seen wherever there was looting or killing. As in certain modern societies, the business people were afraid of the *ayyar*, who, as far as the people of the *suqs* were concerned, were nothing but bandits. They had to be paid off to avoid trouble. The streets were controlled more and more by the *ayyar*. Their unity made them formidable.

We have just spoken of the Nizamiya school, founded by the chief minister of the Seljuks, Nizam al-mulk, who gave the school its name. It stood in the very center of the al-Thalatha *suq*, the Tuesday Market. The Nizamiya, built in 1065, played a dominant and essential role. But in the field of general culture, it suffers by comparison with the intellectual upsurge during the period of the caliph Mamun, which was inspired by an increase in knowledge of the science and philosophy of antiquity. With the founding of the Nizamiya, we are dealing with something completely different. Although the new university doubtless offered solid instruction in Arabic philology, it was mainly a weapon destined to destroy everything not exclusively Sunnite.

There was no question of setting up a type of research institute, such as we imagine the Academy of Wisdom founded by the caliphate to have been. It was to train personnel, who, in life in general and in the administration in particular, would stubbornly defend a certain doctrine and would resolutely place itself in the service of an authoritarian regime. The battle was quickly won, for the doctor of laws for whom the Nizamiya had been founded, Shirazi, was able to proclaim loudly twenty years later, "I have not gone to any city or town without finding one of my students exercising the duties of cadi, secretary, or preacher." This was a religious educational institution dominated by the Shafi'ite rite. It is to the Nizamiya's credit to list among its teachers Ghazali, known as Algazel in the West during the Middle Ages, the great mystic Abd al-Qadir Jilani, whose tomb still exists in Baghdad, and Baha al-din, Saladin's biographer. Among its students were the poet Sa'di and the other biographer of the same Saladin, Imad al-din Isfahani.

We must, therefore, take with a grain of salt certain Persian historians' appreciation of the Seljuks. "They protected scholars, proved themselves to be friends of science, and maintained the respect that was due them. In this way, they obtained excellent results. Indeed, in the entire empire, especially in Iraq and Khurasan, learned men appeared who composed works on jurisprudence, collected religious traditions, and assembled so many books concerning the precise and imprecise verses of the Koran, its commentaries, and the authenticity of traditions, that the root of faith became solidly implanted in hearts." It can be clearly seen why religious quarrels broke out because of the instruction given at this school. There were many adversaries, one of whom wrote this significant threat, "This school destroys true religion and corrupts the original purity of the faithful; it must, therefore, be destroyed!"

Thus, from the time of the founding of the school, a considerable effort was made in favor of the Ash'arite creed, named after its creator, Ash'ari. Like Mutazilism, Ash'arism flourished in Baghdad, where its founder had lived and had been buried. This propaganda zeal exasperated the Hanbalites. Between 1065 and 1082, there were sporadic and lengthy discussions in the mosques. Armored and helmeted troops brutally broke up demonstrations. As early as 1055, disagreements had broken out between the Shafi'ites and the Hanbalites over liturgical questions. In any case, the establishment was looked upon with great favor at the time. For example, during a fire which raged through the neighborhood of the school, the students, at great risk to themselves, saved the books in the library. At the end of the twelfth century, when the caliph Nasir restored the library, precious manuscripts were stored in it. All trace of the building was lost in the first half of the fifteenth century, even though it had been previously restored four times after floods and a fire.

At the very beginning of the Abbasid reign, there was the rise of a new social class, the government scribes, which rapidly gained great influence. The best known writers came from among them. A new group, the seminary professors, came into being with the Seljuk Turks. The former were able to lay down the law, since they were given the duty, or took it themselves, of conserving the purity of morals, even private ones, and the righteousness of thought which was to remain invariable. They declared war against subversive literature. This was the period of autos-da-fé. With these militant literary works, we are far from the free progress inspired by the Abbasid golden age. The Sunnite dogma became more precise as it hardened.

The sometimes violent discussions between Shi'ites and Sunnites did not disappear overnight. They cropped up again at intervals, and they must have tired the commercial people. At the instigation of the police prefect, a compromise was reached in 1050. He had the idea of having the Shi'ite call to prayer proclaimed in the Sunnite section at the Basra Gate, while in Karkh there was a reading of the merits of the Companions of the Prophet. This prefect, who had assumed the task of ending the religious disputes, had to resign because of the brazen activity of the city's thieves. Religious troubles of the same kind began again in the years that followed, and the poor arbitrator was assassinated in 1060. In 1085 and 1095, bloody fights occurred between these two factions of the people of Baghdad. At last, in 1095, writers refer to the final peace between the Shi'ite and Sunnite communities as an important event.

Baghdad spread out on both banks of the river, and each of its parts flourished and degenerated independently. Repairs were not systematically undertaken. The city seemed to be divided into sections which were easily distinguished, because they were separated by devastated areas full of debris. A construction plan was drawn up by the caliph Muqtadi. He built up new areas around which his successor, Mustazhir, set up a wall in 1099. Ibn Jubayr saw what remained of it.

The restoration was necessary since the ramparts built by order of the caliph Musta'in were in ruins. A new wall of baked brick, surrounded by a deep moat, began at the ancient stronghold, went around the Mukharrim section, and turned until it reached the Tigris. Here are the names of the gates of this wall, which was to protect the left bank, going from the north to the south. There was the Shammasiya Gate, or Bab al-Sultan, today called Bab al-Mu'azzam, or even the Imam A'zam Gate, the name given to the old Rusafa neighborhood by Abu Hanifa. This was at the end of Grand Avenue, which ran through the Arcade Gate to the Main Bridge. The ruins of Bab Mu'azzam were completely removed by the city in 1925 in order to widen a street. In the next suburb, between the Shammasiya Gate and the Bab Baradan, there was an area where outdoor prayers were said, the *Mosalla*. This was often the gathering place for rebellious troops. After the Baradan Gate came the Khurasan Gate, more recently called Bab al-Zafariya or Bab Wastani. Then there was the al-Halba Gate, which in the thirteenth century was called the Talisman Gate. It was walled up by order of the Ottoman Sultan Murad IV after the conquest of the city by the Persians. Then there were the Horse Market Gate, the Bab Abraz, and the Gate of the Tuesday Market, where cloth merchants later set up shop. The last is also known as the Bab Basaliya and Bab Kalwadha.

The real capital had been on the left bank for quite some time. The importance of the Round City was a thing of the past found only in books.

Here are some observations which Louis Massignon made while visiting Baghdad. "There has been no diminishing of the walls on the east side of the left bank, to the south of the al-Ghazl [*suq*], where the minaret of the caliph's mosque still rises, beyond the big gardens where European consulates have sprung up in the last fifty years. It is a fact that Mustazhir's restoration in 1095 in no way deformed the original laying out of the wall to the northwest. If there was a slight change in the left-bank wall during the centuries, it was far from being diminished in the northwest; there was an extension toward the northeast and the east. The only point where a text tells of a change was at Bab Abraz, which, according to Yaqut, was well inside the walls, after the annexation of the Zafariya district had moved them farther out, and at Bab Zafariya and Bab Suq al-Thalatha, when the palaces of the caliphate and their gardens were parcelled out after the Mongol conquest and became part of the city." In short, the restoration of 1095, like the later one in 1173, consisted of urgent repairs with no displacement.

In addition to the Nizamiya school, many other monuments were erected or restored in the capital of the caliphate: the Sultan's mosque, Abu Hanifa's tomb, the Tajiya school, and Ma'ruf Karkhi's tomb.

During the first months of his stay in Baghdad, Toghrul-beg lived in the residence of the Buyid prince, Adud al-daula. The building burned down, and, when it was rebuilt, it was renamed *Dar al-Saltana*, the Palace of the Sultan. The new residence was built as a fortified castle. The sultan left an important garrison in the city. This is a good clue to the relationship between the sultanate and the caliphate. The caliph had no real forces at all.

The Sultan's mosque, begun by Malik-Shah, the only Seljuk who had lived permanently in Baghdad, was finished in 1130. Actually, it was only an enlargement and restoration of the Mukharrim neighborhood mosque. The monument, which is no longer standing, existed until the Mongol conquest.

Abu Hanifa's mausoleum has its rightful place in Baghdad. He is honored there as the citizen who created one of the four rites of the Sunnite branch of Islam. His tomb stood in the Rusafa district. It was a superb edifice built in 1067 by the order of a Seljuk vizier. The eleventh-century structure has disappeared; the one that is admired today is a restoration made under the Ottomans in the seventeenth century. This burial mosque received a great deal of care as recently as the last century. It is near the river, not far from what used to be the cemetery of the Abbasid caliphs.

Several years later, in 1086, the minaret of the Dar al-Saltana mosque was finished. It is now the site of the Suq al-Ghazl minaret. Massignon wondered if that tower was not the same as the Seljuk minaret.

The next year, a Seljuk minister, Taj al-mulk, built another school, which never became as famous as the Nizamiya. It was called Tajiya after the name of its founder. It stood near the Bab Abraz, the gate which formed the southeast corner of the wall surrounding the buildings on the east bank. Perhaps it was somewhat forsaken because it was situated in an outlying area. As a matter of fact, in 1252, the authorities routed squatters who had taken up residence in the school and lived there as though they owned it.

Several buildings bearing the name of Tutush, the Sultan Alp-Arslan's son, were constructed in the same period near the Nizamiya school. They included a covered market, a hospital, and a school. These were still flourishing in the following century, according to the geographer Yaqut.

When the Round City was founded, cemeteries were placed outside each of the four gates. In the Seljuk period it was obvious that the situation had been changed by events. On the east bank, north of the Harbiya district and separated from it by a wall, was the Quraish cemetery, formerly called the Syrian Gate cemetery. The most venerated descendants of the Alid family were buried there. Here too was the tomb of the imam Ahmad ibn Hanbal, "the rigid traditionalist, the hero of the juridical persecution of the defenders of the increate Koran," the founder of the Hanbalite rite, which was so popular in Baghdad until the fourteenth century. The tomb was often flooded by the Tigris, was often repaired, and was finally swallowed by the waters. The Shuniziya cemetery was on the west bank. The tomb of the mystic Junaid was located there. The Khaizuran cemetery was in Rusafa and was marked by Abu Hanifa's mausoleum, which is still standing. East of the Basra Gate, there was the cemetery called the Convent Gate cemetery. The tomb of the famous venerated holy man Ma'ruf Karkhi was there. His mausoleum, which had been destroyed by fire in 1067 and was solidly rebuilt in brick and plaster, still stands and is used as a topographical marker on the right bank. Omar Suhrawardi's tomb is in the Wardiya cemetery, near Bab Abraz.

Of course, the markets were moved as the different sections of the city developed. It is not always easy to follow them. Not far from the Gharaba Gate in the walls surrounding the caliph's palaces, near the Tigris, the needle merchants set up shop. Farther toward the east, there was the Gate of the Date Market, and close by there was the cotton building. Long Street, which ran from Bab al-Taq to the Khurasan Gate to the west, was lined along its entire length with shops where various manufactured products were sold. Commercial activity was centered around Bab al-Taq. The perfume merchants lorded it over the others and would not set up shop next to grease dealers or those who sold products that had strong odors. In this area were also rug merchants and second-hand clothing dealers. Between Bab al-Taq and the river were the boot merchants, fowl merchants, and florists. There were also the pleasant shops of the money changers, dealers in rich cloth, food shops, bakeries, and butcher shops. Beyond that was the goldsmiths' center, famous for its beautiful architecture. It was a tall building with teakwood beams that supported overhanging rooms. Not far from there was the Bookdealers' Market, a large area that became a sort of literary circle.

Toward the east, near the Bab al-Taq, which had become basically the small-business section, was located the Yahya Market, already known by Ya'qubi and called the Main Market by the geographer Istakhri. Not far from there was a group of bakery and pastry shops. In the northern part of the caliph's stronghold was the Market of Thirst, already famous for its size in Ya'qubi's time. It was known to be the best supplied of all the markets. Inside these walls were located two markets that were indispensable to military officers and men, the Arms Market and the Horse Market. At the southern end of the east bank was the Tuesday Market. The appearance of the Karkh area had changed. During the Seljuk period, it was known for its beautiful mansions set pleasantly in private gardens, equipped with norias and, in some cases, with balconies overlooking the Tigris. A writer of the time describes the noises of the neighborhood as a medley of the squeaking of the wheels of the bucket elevators, the quacking of ducks, and the various cries of the soldiers and the servants. The description is proof that the markets which had formerly been located there had been moved elsewhere.

At this time, Baghdad produced cotton cloth, silk materials, matting, shaped crystal, glass, ointments, potions, and electuaries. These were the principal exports. Baghdad ciclatoun continued to be highly prized.

No building of this period or of previous periods remains which could, through its inscriptions, give some idea of the relative power of the caliph and his "protectors." On the other hand, the monumental epigraphy of adjacent areas

tells us precisely of the authority of the neighboring prince-
lings, who, after the break with the west and the coming to
power of the Fatimids in Cairo and Syria, owed absolutely
no allegiance to the Abbasid caliph. Here are some new
indications of this situation. The Marwanid lords, who took
over Upper Mesopotamia to the detriment of the Buyids,
found no reason to mention the caliph or even the Seljuk
sultan in their inscriptions. This was especially true in
Diyarbekir. In any event, in the Damascus texts engraved on
the Umayyad mosque in 1082, the Seljuks were placed under
the protection of the caliph of the Abbasid empire, especially
under that of the caliph Muqtadi. The announcement is no
more or less than an election poster declaring that the Syrian
capital was no longer under Fatimid domination. This
Seljuk gesture had no follow-up, and later inscriptions in
Aleppo make no mention of the existence of a caliph. The
Marwanids alone still recognized caliphs with high-sound-
ing titles, such as "the glorified lord and very great king of
kings."

We shall leave the Great Seljuks with the enthusiastic,
but slightly melancholy, description by Khatib Baghdadi,
who died in 1071. "There is no city in the world equal to
Baghdad in the abundance of its riches, the importance of its
business, the number of its scholars and important people,
the distinction of its leaders and its common people, the
extent of its districts, the width of its boundaries, the great
number of its palaces, inhabitants, streets, avenues, alleys,
mosques, baths, docks and caravansaries, the purity of its
air, the sweetness of its water, the freshness of its dew and
its shade, the temperateness of its summer and winter, the
healthfulness of its spring and fall, and its great swarming
crowds. The buildings and the inhabitants were most
numerous during the time of Harun al-Rashid, when the

city and its surrounding areas were full of cooled rooms, thriving places, fertile pastures, rich watering-places for ships. Then the riots began, an uninterrupted series of misfortunes befell the inhabitants, its flourishing condition came to ruin to such an extent that, before our time and the century preceding ours, it found itself, because of the perturbation and the decadence it was experiencing, in complete opposition to all capitals and in contradiction to all inhabited countries."

We should pay homage to Khatib Baghdadi, who did an overwhelming amount of work. In his voluminous history of Baghdad, he gave the biographies of all the famous men who passed through Baghdad and, of course, of those who lived there. He wrote a valuable preface to that work, thanks to which we have topographical information about the city. Although he covered just a very short period, no author, whether poet or prose writer, surpasses him in his ability as a compiler or in knowledge.

We should extend our gratitude to Ibn Bawwab, a decorator, painter of frescoes, and especially a calligrapher, who died in 1022. He became famous as the inventor of a new form of art writing, first started by Ibn Muqla, who died in 939. For a time, he was a librarian in Shiraz.

8.

UNSTABLE BALANCE

GEORGE MAKDISI WROTE: "The Seljuk period, like the Buyid, was characterized by a power struggle between the caliph and the sultan, a struggle to which they devoted their greatest efforts. In time, Baghdad suffered from it. This does not mean that the difficulties in its socio-economic life can be attributed directly and solely to this very real situation; for Baghdad was always exposed to damage of a physical nature: torrential rains, strong winds, hail, drought, locusts. To damage of a physical nature should be added damage of a political nature: invasions, illegal taxes, looting, burning. There was more destruction than construction. The city and most of its inhabitants suffered a great deal from famine, cannibalism, epidemics, epizootic, crime, and vice."

The decadence of the Great Seljuks in Baghdad can be placed at the time of the death of Malik-Shah in 1092. The caliphs then anxiously witnessed the ups and downs of the battles waged between the competing members of the Seljuk family and the lords of the Baghdad suburbs. Nothing was ever definitely settled, and authority was constantly challenged anew.

The caliph still remained in danger in Baghdad because of the surprising activity of the Batinites, called Assassins in Europe. During the first half of the twelfth century, the caliph was, beyond any doubt, the weakest of all political figures.

When we speak of decadence, it should be remembered that the reference is to Baghdad and not to the Moslem world. The Mesopotamian city was affected financially by the dismemberment of the empire and politically by the decrease in the caliph's authority.

During this period, the caliph tried in every way to regain the upper hand. Ibn Jubayr read the names of the caliphs Muqtafi and Mustadi on the doors of the Ka'ba in Mecca. In Damascus, two inscriptions from the year 1109, placed side by side, bear witness to this competition, since one names the caliph alone and the other names only the Seljuk sultan. These are the last Syrian inscriptions to mention an Abbasid caliph.

The fragmentary text engraved on the minaret in Saweh, Persia, in 1118, is the culminating point of this attempt at balance. One line is reserved for the Seljuk sultan and another for the Abbasid caliph, whose titles, borrowed from Fatimid protocol, include a new and unusual expression: "the slave, the friend, and the caliph of God." Actually the expression "caliph of Allah" was seen in titles composed several years previously.

The Inalid family succeeded the Marwanids in Mesopotamia and recognized only the Seljuks from 1117 on.

According to a text of the eleventh century, Baghdad was at that time divided into four districts, "each of which equaled a large city in area."

Beginning with the reign of Muqtadi, the area reserved for the sovereigns was beautified with new buildings. Even with the Badr Gate, on both sides of the wall surrounding the caliph's palaces, there was the Perfumers' Market, *suq al-raihaniyin,* where a great variety of flowers and fruits were sold. The market surrounded a large undeveloped area. In 1113, the caliph Mustazhir had a new palace built on this site. In order to do this, he had to do away with some small markets, consisting of no more than one hundred shops, which had been set up in the caliph's enclosed area. The new castle was an immense structure containing about sixty rooms. Succeeding caliphs lived there until the Mongol conquest. Later, in 1162, Mustazhir's grandson, Mustanjid added a belvedere, which was admired by Ibn Jubayr.

Before going on to the rather significant political events, we should examine the incidents, either by chance or provoked by rioters, which harried the lives of the people of Baghdad. Both series of events will be given in chronological order.

In 1092, a fire broke out which enveloped the entire Mu'alla canal district. It destroyed the money-changers' markets and the *suqs* of the goldsmiths and of the dealers in dried fruit and fragrant flowers. The fire was quickly controlled, but the damage was very great. In 1100, a fire, fanned by a strong wind, destroyed most of a neighborhood. It reached some of the caliph's palaces near the Gate of the People in the Mukharrim wall. In 1102, a fire damaged a neighborhood in the southeastern part of the east city, in the vicinity of the Mu'alla canal.

In 1106, a terrible flood inundated the east bank, destroying grain storehouses and damaging several palaces inside Mukharrim. A new fire broke out in 1108, inside the same walls. It grew so large that the inhabitants fled, broke holes in the ramparts near the Abraz Gate, and took refuge in a nearby cemetery. That same year a second fire broke out and spread panic among the people who were threatened with famine. There were some deaths, and many buildings were damaged. In 1114, a fire destroyed the area around the Badr Gate in the wall surrounding the caliph's palaces.

In 1117, an earthquake destroyed many houses on the west bank. In 1118, a new fire raged through the Perfumers' Market as well as the neighboring markets. In 1134, fire broke out in several places in the city and a large part of the *suqs* was destroyed. The merchants lost almost all their goods. In 1146, the palace built by the caliph Mustarshid was ruined by fire. The caliph Muqtafi had just arrived to spend three days in the company of his favorites. The fire was caused by a servant's careless handling of a candle. Everything was destroyed, but there were no deaths. To show his gratitude, the caliph distributed great sums in alms and ordered the freeing of many prisoners.

The Palace of the Crown was lost as the result of a fire in 1154; it was to be rebuilt by the caliph Mustadi in 1178. In 1179, a flood caused a general catastrophe. The walls of the western part of the city were ripped open, and the water flowed into various districts. All of that side of the city was under water. The inhabitants tried desperately to get to the other bank. Those who took them across charged exorbitant rates. The right bank was not spared either, especially the Harbiya cemetery, where the tomb of Ibn Hanbal was located. There was another flood in 1173 which covered several neighborhoods and damaged the Nizamiya school.

In 1174, the worst catastrophe of this period struck. Ibn al-Athir writes that the rain poured down and the Tigris overflowed its banks, causing a flood. The water level reached eighteen inches higher than the maximum recorded since the founding of the city. The people did everything they could to ward off disaster, including filling in the holes with earth as they appeared in the dikes. Water flooded the Adud al-daula hospital; boats entered the building through windows whose shutters had been carried off by the flood. A mosque in the Karkh district was also flooded when a hastily erected protecting dike gave way. That was all that was needed to turn the inhabitants of the neighborhood against the people of the Basra Gate for an entire week, just as in the past.

Disorder in the streets went on as usual. In 1100, the disruption of the *ayyar* became intolerable, and the caliph decided to act with exceptional severity. Instigators of a riot were arrested, and many others fled. Uprisings took place again in 1104. Several years later, writers note an extraordinary event, the apparent and temporary reconciliation of the Shi'ites and the Sunnites. The Shi'ites felt that they had been weakened by the battlefield death of the lord of Hillah, a professed Shi'ite, and the salutary effect led to appeasement, something that all the efforts of Baghdad's rulers had never been able to accomplish. The people of Karkh allowed a procession of Sunnite pilgrims to pass through on their way to the tomb of a Companion of the Prophet; in turn, a group of Shi'ites were able to visit calmly the tomb of one of their imams. In 1110, the *ayyar* overcame a police contingent that had come to disperse them on the left bank of the river. The two hundred members of the police force had to be mobilized to stop the looting. In 1118, a revolution almost broke out after a bargeman was killed by the prefect of police guards. The *ayyar* participated in this uprising. The soldiers pitilessly attacked the brigands, forcing them to cross the river, and more people were drowned than were killed in the actual battle.

It would take too long to tell in detail of the terrible dissension that occurred among the Seljuk princes immediately after the death of Malik-Shah in 1092, but brief mention should be made since the discord gives evidence of the physical and moral incapacity of the caliph, the theoretical master of Baghdad. Battles in the open country succeeded the political intrigues headed by Turkan Khatun, Malik-Shah's astute widow. Malik-Shah's oldest son, Barkiyaruq, was more or less recognized as the new caliph, and he had his name included in the public prayer. His success was rather precarious since, in order to consolidate his position, he had to defeat the army of his uncle, Tutush (1095), who had occupied Baghdad for a short period. Barqiyaruq also had to fight his brother Muhammed, who succeeded in having some of the caliph's troops desert and make Barkiyaruq admit to his, Muhammed's, supremacy. Barkiyaruq was not discouraged, however; he recruited new troops and descended on Baghdad. After several indecisive battles, a peace treaty was drawn up and Barkiyaruq's pre-eminence was recognized.

In 1123, the lord of Hillah's Bedouins attacked Baghdad. The Seljuks' help saved the caliph Mustarshid, who, in order to defend his capital, had to resort to mass conscription. Shortly, however, the Abbasid monarch was no longer able to count on the Seljuks' assistance, since they became his enemies. The caliph thought he could strengthen his defenses by increasing the thickness of the walls of his stronghold and decreasing the number of gates to four.

There were other local chieftains in the area. Their proliferation gives the clearest evidence of the weakening of Seljuk power and of the caliph's authority.

Lack of unity among the Seljuks encouraged the caliph. Mustarshid did not hesitate to recruit an army to oppose his adversaries: the Seljuk prince, the Zangid prince of Mosul, and the Arab lord of Hillah. A few words are in order regarding this Arab master of the city of Hillah, northwest of Baghdad on the Euphrates. "He was an ostentatious man and patron of numerous dependents. He knew how to protect and defend. Every day was a holiday for him, and, in his time, Hillah was a place to which men flocked from everywhere, a refuge for the unfortunate who went there full of hope, an asylum for the banished and the frightened exile."

Petty arguments of the time did harm to the spirit of Islam. While the conquering Turks were increasing the territory of Islam by their advance and their settlement in Asia Minor, to the detriment of the Byzantines, the caliph and, in general, the people of Baghdad became disinterested in the renewed warlike spirit of the Moslems. The situation was similar to that when the Crusades threatened Islamic heritage. The repeated appeals of the Syrians and their leaders for battle against the Crusaders had little effect on the official circles of the caliph or the sultan in Baghdad, who remained quite indifferent. The first step took place after the fall of Antioch: "Syrian envoys presented themselves at the court of Baghdad, with their heads shaved, weeping, crying out in distress; the speech of a cadi brought tears to the eyes of those who were present." And that was all! Petitions from Syria sent in the first years of the twelfth century had no more effect than had the visit by the Syrians. The following scene occurred in 1110. A group of envoys from Aleppo, accompanied by holy men of the city, noisily entered the Mosque of the Caliphs. When they became aware of a wedding procession of a Seljuk princess passing through the city with a scandalous display of luxury, they became more vociferous and shouted even more loudly. Seljuk troops headed toward the demonstrators, but were quickly diverted to Mosul to put down some rebels. The caliph was cautious in his dealings with the sultan, who, although weakened, was still dangerous. It was probably against Turkish power that the caliph Mustazhir had new walls erected around the entire city. He certainly also wanted to protect himself against the covetousness of the nearby petty chiefs, made daring by Seljuk weakness and the caliph's inaction.

The caliph Mustarshid, who finally succeeded in recruiting an army, used it to protect himself against the neighboring marauding emirs, whose troops were guilty of looting, especially in 1122. The next year, the caliph actually left on an expedition against the famous lord of Hillah, who was in open rebellion. The dissension lasted until the end of the caliph's reign in 1135. In the meantime, secret meetings had taken place, without any appreciable results, between the caliph, the Seljuk sultan, and the little emirs of Iraq. In the midst of the petty squabbles among all these rivals, the caliph remained neutral, through either helplessness or indifference.

From the point of view of general history, for the most part, the caliphate and the people of Baghdad were passive regarding the aggression of the Crusaders. The breaking up of the empire, which had been taking place for two centuries, contributed to the lack of public interest. One lone historian assures us, however, that the caliph Muqtafi (1135–60) later sent an army of twenty thousand men to participate in the battle against the Franks. We know no more than that.

In January, 1127, the Seljuk sultan Mahmud and the caliph Mustarshid confronted each other. The caliph's troops, stationed on the left bank of the Tigris, were attacked by the sultan's army. One thousand of the sultan's men invaded the caliph's palace and looted it. An annalist of the time was present at the flight of the female personnel. But the caliph's militia, supported by the shouting and screaming people, recaptured the lost territory and sacked the sultan's palace. They hooted the sultan in the streets and shouted, "Aren't you ashamed, Batinite, to fight the caliph, while you let the Franks and the Greeks do as they please?"

The misunderstanding between the caliph and the Seljuk sultan's successor, his brother Mas'ud, grew even worse and resulted in another armed conflict. In 1134, Mustarshid became quite worried because of Mas'ud's ambition, which he decided to thwart by readying an army to attack the sultan. Mustarshid had learned that the sultan was planning to march on Baghdad, to destroy and plunder it. Once again, it would probably be an exaggeration to speak of a struggle between the clergy and the empire. The caliph set out with indescribable pomp at the head of a large army, a considerable crowd gathering to see this impressive spectacle. During the battle, a number of Turkish troops betrayed the caliph, who was soon abandoned and taken prisoner. The people of Baghdad, quickly informed, did not lose the opportunity of taking to the streets to do their usual looting. The demonstration took on anti-Shi'ite overtones. Talks took place, and, upon the insistence of the Khurasan Sindjar, the Sultan of Iraq freed the caliph and gave him back his titles with the understanding that he would promise never to raise an army again. Finally, the Batinites assassinated the caliph in Maragha, in Azerbaijan. There is reason to believe that the murder was instigated by the Seljuk. The sultan had the caliph buried in a splendid mausoleum.

Once again Baghdad was besieged, and Mustarshid's son and successor, Rashid, an abandoned and fugitive monarch, sought allies but never found any loyal ones. Indeed, difficulties continued with the Seljuk sultan, Mas'ud, who surrounded and looted the caliph's palace in order to pay himself a sum that had been promised by Mustarshid. The Seljuk was thrown back, and the caliph thought that all danger had been averted. The neighboring lords helped the caliph but were not able to stop the victorious offensive and return of the sultan. Rashid was dispossessed, wandered about from Mosul to Ispahan, and was finally assassinated.

The relatively clear sequence of events just reviewed seems decidedly petty. Arab historians themselves are perturbed by all of this. One says, "When no goal could be reached, no wish fulfilled, and there was nothing left to do but fight, retreat seemed necessary."

The coming to power of Rashid's nephew, Muqtafi, solved nothing. The sultan Mas'ud held Muqtafi under his thumb. The sultan had this message sent to him: "Let me know what you and all those you are responsible for need so that I can assign you land grants, whose income will provide for these needs." This was true slavery!

Then the last call for help came from the Moslem chiefs who were at war with the Franks. The appeal came from Zangi, the prince of Aleppo, in 1138. The Arab writers' account is interesting for more than one reason, for it at least reveals the way mass demonstrations were organized in Baghdad. Once again the cry for help was to no avail. Zangi sent the cadi, Ibn Shahrazuri, to Baghdad to plead especially with the Seljuk sultan, Mas'ud, and to point out the danger in delay, since all that stood between the Greeks and the sultan was the city of Aleppo. If that city were to be taken, the Greeks would come down the Euphrates and harass the sultan right in Baghdad. Ibn Shahrazuri says that he gave the following instructions to the representative of the Baghdad cadi: "Take these pieces of gold; distribute them among the people, whether they be inhabitants of Baghdad or foreigners. Friday, when the preacher will have climbed up into the pulpit, direct these men to stand up and cry in a single voice, 'Help Islam! Help the religion of Mohammed!' Let them then leave the mosque and head toward the sultan's palace, while asking for his support. I posted another man who was to do the same thing in the sultan's mosque. When Friday came, at the very moment that the preacher was climbing up into the pulpit, the cadi of Aleppo arose, tore his clothes, threw off his turban, and began to shout. All those present joined him with their cries and their tears. There was no one in the mosque who had not risen to his feet while weeping. The service was interrupted. Everyone then headed toward the sultan's palace. The entire population of Baghdad and all the soldiers gathered in front of the palace, breaking into tears and crying out for help. Nothing could restrain the movement. The sultan trembled in his palace."

In 1148, violence broke out as the result of an uprising of Bedouin bands, who had been recruited by the nobles of neighboring regions. Five thousand horsemen arrived in Baghdad, and, taking advantage of a time when the city's garrison was neglected, launched an attack, captured the caliph's residence, and went wild. A street battle took the lives of about five hundred men, among whom were patrolling soldiers. Such raids on Baghdad, which were recurrent at this period of Seljuk helplessness, can be attributed less to political whims of the chiefs than to the audacity of looting rioters.

In order to oppose such assailants, the caliph Muqtafi mobilized conscripted soldiers and mercenaries who succeeded in ridding Baghdad of the criminals. Then by order of the caliph, the ramparts were repaired, two of the gates were walled up, ditches were dug, and fortifications were built. The caliph ordered the important people, the merchants, and the leaders of the city to contribute the cash necessary for carrying out this work. It was a forced loan. The Arab annalists tell us that it created great hardship among the people.

In 1157, the city of Baghdad suffered another siege, the fourth from the time it was founded. Once again, there was a fight between the Seljuk sultan, Muhammad II, and the caliph Muqtafi, who wanted to shake off the yoke of his demanding masters. When the caliph refused to include the sultan's name in public prayers, the Seljuk army marched on Baghdad and took over the city. The caliph decided to defend himself with all his strength. After destroying the pontoon bridge, he withdrew within the walls surrounding the palace. The battle raged. The caliph's army used heavy machines, catapults, and mangonels as well as burning projectiles. They fought even on the Tigris. The sultan rebuilt the pontoon bridge and got a foothold on the east bank, blocking the Crown Palace where the caliph had accumulated a large stock of rations and ammunition. The fact that the caliph promised five dinars to every wounded man shows that he was hard pressed. As a result of the offer, a great number of slightly wounded men came to claim their bonus. There was a shortage of food for the civilian population. The sultan ordered ladders to be set up so that his men could climb over the outside walls, an unnecessary effort since the people of Baghdad opened the gates. One part of the Seljuk army was commanded by the Zangid prince of Mosul, who was beginning to be disgusted by this fight among Moslems. In addition, a caravan of pilgrims, returning from Mecca, did not hesitate to show their indignation and anger at this civil war. It is possible that a bribe by the caliph may have had something to do with the Mesopotamian prince's lack of enthusiasm. In addition, Sultan Muhammad had learned of a plot against him. During the blockade, which lasted two months, many buildings were destroyed, and the people of Baghdad, who had suffered greatly from hunger, were attacked by an epidemic.

Later, a revolt against the caliph Mustadi (1170–80) was instigated by the chief of the Turkish militia. The caliph was besieged in his palace and, as a last resort, climbed out on a terrace and cried for help. The people surrounded the palace, freed the caliph, and routed the plotters. During Mustadi's reign, the people were particularly stirred up. There was, for example, a savage demonstration against a Shi'ite poet who had been condemned by a religious tribunal. Followed by a brick-throwing crowd, the poor man panicked and jumped into the Tigris. His body was fished out and dragged through the city's markets.

After the Seljuk period, the land, with the exception of Asia Minor, was governed by regents. Baghdad, ruled by the caliph, was just one of a swarm of principalities. One can understand the disdain with which the caliph treated outside events, which took place so far from the Mesopotamian city. Let everyone look out for his own territory! The caliph was happy just handing out positions, titles, and robes of honor to his followers.

According to a commentator on a text by Ibn Hauqal, "a cathedral mosque was built on the west bank. The only things remaining today in that dilapidated neighborhood are this mosque, the Quraish cemetery, and the district named after the Abu Hanifa mausoleum. Construction was begun on another site, near the Mu'alla Canal. This new neighborhood was surrounded by a solid and powerful wall, outside of which there circled a deep moat supplied with water from the Tigris."

The geographer Idrisi, who died in 1165, merely repeats the details of the founding of the ancient city. He adds that there were two bridges and that he thought the west bank was remarkable because it was covered with gardens and orchards.

Claude Cahen wrote: "The cultural life of Baghdad in that period concerned itself with the past and with changing times. In spite of the looting, great library facilities remain. It is one of the great centers for pilgrimages and, at all times, for scholars of every type, very few of whom have not visited it. It can boast of literary works, such as Hariri's *Maqamat*, at the beginning of the century."

Indeed, Hariri is the outstanding literary figure of the time. He attempted to beautify the *Seances* of his predecessor, Hamadani. Speakers of Arabic really do consider Hariri a master. For us, Hariri's *Seances* represents the staggering gymnastics of overelaborate language, full of unbelievable difficulties, which seems affected, a true delirium of words. The writer is swallowed up by his virtuosity. Arab critics, however, think *Seances* highly successful. One of them compliments Hariri for having taken full advantage of the rich imagery and mystery of the language.

The great thinker of the century was certainly Ghazali. Although he was a wanderer, he should be mentioned in connection with Baghdad since he taught at the Nizamiya school. His fame, which was well merited, spread to Europe. Before him, Qushairi, a mystic who died in 1074, tried to prove that Sufism did not contradict orthodoxy and was in accord with Ash'ari's position. Sufism had had its saints in the city for a long time. We have had occasion, for example, to mention Hallaj and Ma'ruf Karkhi several times. There were many commemorative monuments to these people. The originality of the highly moral thought of Ghazali, whose life was incomparably noble, consisted in the repudiation of all the philosophical and skeptical tendencies to which he was led, with some distaste, by his erudition. A brief explanation will show the kind of scholars Ghazali opposed. The philosophical movement begun by Kindi became even more important with Farabi and reached its culmination with Avicenna, who died in 1037. (Avicenna is not discussed here because he never visited Baghdad.) Ghazali was concerned with halting the drift toward disunion and toward rationalist doctrines which were warping the spirit of Islam. He did not want religious faith and life to depend for their existence upon scientific systems, which are subject to constant change and difference of opinion. He felt the danger in petty, barren quibbling. He encouraged piety through observance of the cult. Indeed, Ghazali represents an important moment in Sufism, for, with him, there was no wandering from orthodoxy. It is interesting that a chapter of his *The Revival of the Religious Sciences* is entitled "Fundamental Values in the Reading of the Koran."

Abd al-Qadir Jilani (1166), an extremely popular holy man, the oldest founder of the brotherhood, was most effective through his simple and clear sermons. Posterity was right in revering him. The city of Baghdad still maintains his mausoleum with great care. Thanks to this holy man there was a proliferation of monasteries from the thirteenth century on.

9.

THE GOLDEN TWILIGHT AND OBLIVION

BAGHDAD HAD BEEN NOTHING MORE than a regional capital for a long time before the breaking up of the Seljuk family. After the departure of these Turkish masters, the caliph fancied himself the uncontested sovereign of the provincial city. For the caliphate, it was a new golden age of somewhat reduced proportions. The caliph believed he was the only administrative and military chief. But everything is relative, and Baghdad was merely the center of a phantom caliphate, despite the feeble attempts at sovereignty that we shall examine.

The new emancipation began in the middle of the eleventh century. An inscription in Mecca mentions the caliph of Baghdad alone at this time. It is the first authentic document, but we know through the chronicles that the caliph Mustazhir began the *khutba* privilege without mentioning any other powerful person. We should not forget the activity of one of Muqtafi's ministers, Ibn Hubaira, who became vizier in 1149. Nikita Elisseeff said of him: "His politics was of Hanbalite inspiration. Its goal was the triumph of Sunna, the elimination of political Shi'ism, and the restoration of the temporal and spiritual authority of the Abbasid Caliphate. For that reason, in the east, Ibn Hubaira

135

was busy trying to liberate the caliph from the weakened hold of the last of the Seljuks, while, in the west, he sought an alliance with Nur-al-din, the prince of Aleppo, and encouraged him to undertake the conquest of Egypt."

In 1165, Benjamin of Tudela, not concerned with general politics, spoke of "the great city and the royal residence of the Caliph al Abbasi of the family of Mohammed. He is at the head of the Mohammedan religion, and all the kings of Islam obey him; he occupies a similar position to that held by the Pope over the Christians. He has a place in Bagdad three miles in extent wherein is a great park with all varieties of trees, fruit-bearing and otherwise, and all manners of animals. The whole is surrounded by a wall, and in the park there is a lake whose waters are fed by the River Hiddekel. Whenever the king desires to indulge in recreation and to rejoice and feast, his servants catch all manner of birds, game and flesh, and he goes to his palace with his counsellors and princes. . . .

"Within the domains of the palace of the Caliph there are great buildings of marble and columns of silver and gold, and carvings upon rare stones are fixed in the walls. In the Caliph's palace are great riches and towers filled with gold, silken garments and all precious stones. He does not issue forth from his palace save once in the year, at the feast which the Muhammedans call El-id-bed [*sic*] Ramazan, and they come from distant lands that day to see him. He rides on a mule and is attired in the royal robes of gold and silver and fine linen; on his head is a turban adorned with precious stones of priceless value, and over the turban is a black shawl as a sign of his modesty, implying that all this glory will be covered by darkness on the day of his death. . . . He proceeds from his palace to the great mosque of Islam which is by the Bassorah Gate. Along the road the walls are adorned with silk and purple, and the inhabitants receive him with all kinds of song and exultation. . . . Afterwards he leaves the mosque and returns alone to his palace by way of the river, and the grandees of Islam accompany him in ships on the river until he enters. He does not return the way he came. . . .

"He built, on the other side of the river, on the banks of an arm of the Euphrates which there borders the city, a hospital consisting of blocks of houses and hospices for the sick poor who come to be healed. Here there are about sixty physicians' stores which are provided from the Caliph's house with drugs and whatever else may be required. Every sick man who comes is maintained at the Caliph's expense and is medically treated. Here is a building which is called Dar-al-Maristan, where they keep charge of the demented people who have become insane in the towns through the great heat in the summer, and chain each of them in iron chains until their reason becomes restored to them in the winter-time. Whilst they abide there, they are provided with food from the house of the Caliph; and when their reason is restored they are dismissed and each one of them goes to his house and his home. Money is given to those who have stayed in the hospice on their return to their homes."

The Spanish pilgrim Ibn Jubayr stayed in Baghdad five days in 1184, four years after the succession to the throne of the caliph Nasir, who reigned for forty-five years. We are indebted to Ibn Jubayr for several notes, which are interesting despite their brevity. As can be seen, he broaches his subject with no illusions. "Bagdad is an ancient city, and although it has never ceased to be the capital of the Abbasside Caliphate and the pivot of the Quraishite . . . most of its traces have gone, leaving only a famous name. In comparison with its former state, before misfortune struck it and the eyes of adversity turned towards it, it is like an effaced ruin, a remain washed out, or the statue of a ghost." He expresses his enthusiasm for the river in lyrical terms. "The Tigris which runs between its eastern and its western parts like a mirror shining between two frames, or like a string of pearls between two breasts. And the beauty of the Harim wrought between its water and its air, is celebrated and talked of through the lands." He spends time describing the caliph himself: "The Caliph would sometimes be seen in boats on the Tigris, and sometimes he would go into the desert to hunt. He goes forth in modest circumstance in order to conceal his state from the people, but despite this concealment his fame only increases. We saw this Caliph in the western part in front of his belvedere there. He had come down from it and went up the river in a boat to his palace high on the east bank. He is a youth in years, with a fair beard that is short but full of handsome shape and good to look on, of fair skin, medium stature, and comely aspect. He is about five and twenty years of age. He wore a white dress like a full-sleeved gown, embroidered with gold, and on his head was a gilded cap encircled with black fur of the costly and precious kind used for royal clothes."

But he makes no special case of the caliph. For Ibn Jubayr, the great hero of Islam is evidently Saladin. And he probably knew that the attempts of the western Moslems to enlist the aid of the caliph of Baghdad against the Crusaders were unsuccessful.

During the days that he spent in the Mesopotamian capital, Ibn Jubayr walked about very little. He spent most of his time listening to sermons. He visited pious Sufis and learned theologians, among whom was the polygrapher Ibn Jauzi, who had "a sermon given beside his house on the eastern bank of the river. Adjoining, with its extremity, the palaces of the Caliph, it is near to the Bab al-Basaliya, the last of the gates on the eastern side of the city." We would have preferred a description of the famous Nizamiya school which he visited. He states, at least, that a scholastic movement was being developed, side by side with the more independent movement of the Sufis, with fervent followers "shaken with emotion."

Ibn Jubayr was impressed with the flourishing appearance of the suburbs closest to the city, "passing into the city through gardens and meadows of which all description must fall short." The beauty of the caliph's neighborhood is well described, but it is the only optimistic note in his discussion of the city. "It has no beauty that attracts the eye, or calls him who is restless to depart to neglect his business and to gaze."

As we have said many times, the Round City had been nothing but a myth for a long time. Construction had extended on the other side of the Tigris. Ibn Jubayr describes it thus: "This city has two parts, an eastern and a western, and the Tigris passes between them. Its western part is wholly overcome by ruin. It was the first part to be populated, and the eastern part was but recently inhabited. Nevertheless, despite the ruins, it contains seventeen quarters, each quarter being a separate town. Each has two or three baths, and in eight of them is a congregational mosque where the Friday prayers are said. The largest of these quarters is al-Quraya, on the banks of the Tigris and near to the bridge. This bridge has been carried away by the river in its flood, and the people had turned to crossing by boats. These boats were beyond count; the people, men and women, who night and day continuously cross in recreation are likewise numberless." This had been mentioned before. Khatib Baghdadi had already pointed it out, although he exaggerated the considerable number of boats used as ferries.

Ibn Jubayr continues, "Ordinarily, and because of the many people, the river had two bridges, one near the palaces of the Caliph, and the other above it. The crossings on the boats are now ceaseless."

This pinpoints things for us, for the Quraya neighborhood was situated on the west bank of the river, to the west of the caliph's palaces.

Ibn Jubayr speaks of the Karkh district. "[It] has in it the mosque of Mansur. It is a large mosque, anciently built, and embellished. The Suq al-Maristan itself is a small city and contains the famous Baghdad Hospital. It is on the Tigris, and every Monday and Thursday physicians visit it to examine the state of the sick, and to prescribe for them what they may need. At their disposal are persons who undertake the preparation of the foods and medicines. The hospital is a large palace, with chambers and closets and all the appurtenances of a royal dwelling. Water comes into it from the Tigris." He is speaking of the hospital founded by the Buyid prince Adud al-daula.

Our traveler continues: "In the western part of the city are the orchards and the walled-in gardens whence are brought fruits to the eastern part. This to-day is the home of the Caliph, and that is honour and circumstance enough for it. The Caliph's palaces lie at its periphery and comprise a quarter or more of it, for all the Abbassides live in sumptuous confinement in these palaces, neither going forth nor being seen, and having a settled stipend. A large part of these palaces is used by the Caliph, and he has taken the high belvederes, the splendid halls, and the delightful gardens.

"Another quarter is that called Attabiya, where are made the clothes from which it takes its name, they being of silk and cotton in various colors. Then comes Harbiya, which is the highest on the river bank and beyond which is nothing but the villages outside Bagdad. Other quarters there are that it would take too long to mention. In one of them is the tomb of Ma'ruf Karkhi, a pious man and famed amongst the saints. Also on the west side is the tomb of Musa ibn Ja'far. Many other tombs there are of saints and men of piety and men of noble forebears. To the east of the town, on an eminence outside it, is a large quarter beside the quarter of Rusafa, where, on the bank, was the famous Bab al-Taq. In this quarter is a shrine, superbly built, with a white dome rising into the air, containing the tomb of the imam Abu Hanifa. Near this quarter is the tomb of the imam Ahmad ibn Hanbal and also in this part is the tomb of Hallaj.

"The eastern part of the city has magnificent markets, is arranged on the grand scale and enfolds a population that none could count save God. It has three congregational mosques, in all of which the Friday prayers are said. The Caliph's mosque, which adjoins the palace, is vast and has large water containers and many and excellent conveniences, that is, for the ritual ablutions and cleaning. The mosque of the Sultan is outside the city, and adjoins the palaces also named after the Sultan known as the Shah an Shah. He had been the controller of the affairs of the ancestors of this Caliph and had lived there, and the mosque had been built in front of his residence. The third mosque, that of Rusafa, is in the eastern part, and between it and the mosque of the Sultan lies about a mile. In Rusafa is the sepulchre of the Abbasid caliphs. The full number of congregational mosques in Bagdad, where Friday prayers are said, is eleven.

"The ordinary mosques in both the eastern and western parts cannot be estimated, much less counted. The colleges are about thirty, and all in the eastern part; and there is not one of them that does not outdo the finest palace. The greatest and most famous of them is the Nizamiya.

"The baths in the city cannot be counted.

"The eastern part has four gates: first that on the high part of the bank, the Bab al-Sultan; then Bab Zafariya, then Bab Halba; and then Bab Basaliya. There are the gates in the walls that surrounded the city from the high to the low parts of the bank and wind around it in a long semicircle. Inside, in the markets, are many gates."

It seems evident that in Ibn Jubayr's time many of the gates had been walled up. Bab al-Sultan corresponds to Bab Shammasiya. Bab Zafariya was a new name for Bab Khurasan, today called Bab Wastani. Bab Halba was later called the Talisman Gate. Bab Basaliya, also called Bab Kalwadha, the closest gate to the Tigris, seems to be the same as the Gate of the Tuesday Market, known today as Bab Sharqi.

Although Ibn Jubayr never stopped praising the scholars he met, he is extremely hard on the inhabitants in general: "As to the people, you scarce can find among them any who do not affect, but who yet are vain and proud. Strangers they despise, and they show scorn and disdain to their inferiors, while the stories and news of other men they belittle. Each conceives, in belief and thought, that the whole world is but trivial in comparison with his land, and over the face of the world they find no noble place of living save their own. It is as if they are persuaded that God has no lands or people save theirs. They trail their skirts trippingly and with insolence, turning not, in deference to God from that of which he disapproves, deeming that the highest glory consists in trailing one's mantle, and knowing not that the garment, in accordance to tradition, shall go to the flames."

To counteract this wicked indictment, we should cite the very compromising judgment of the Persian geographer

Mustaufi. "The people here are fair-skinned, good looking, easygoing and pleasant tempered, but slothfulness dominates their nature, and they pass their time in pleasure. Life is made easy to the rich by abundant comforts, whatever is needed for good living can easily be come by, while the poor with a few copper coins can get of a sufficiency for contentment. Most of the people here are fat in body."

With the help of several collections of proverbs, Louis Massignon paints a portrait of the average Baghdadi, with his "ironic and calm demoralization, a resignation to the worst which is at the base of the peoples' soul, in which the rough endurance of the Bedouin is mixed with the intelligent weakness, the gracious suppleness of the Persian."

In order to understand even better how the people of Baghdad thought, we should study these meaningful lines by the same orientalist: "In Moslem Baghdad, whether we are talking of the set phrases of the pedlar at an auction in the souks, the familiar gibes at the canonists in the mosques, schools, and tribunals, the witty words and the songs in the salons and the baths, the theopathic expressions of hermits in uninhabited areas and cemeteries, everything in this city of Islam is transmitted under the sign of religious tradition and prophetic revelation."

Several parts of Ibn Jubayr's description lend themselves to comparisons with certain lines of *The Thousand and One Nights*, full of beautiful local color. We can get from them a good idea of the countryside around Baghdad at the end of the twelfth century. The descriptions taken from the *Tale of Nur al-Din and Anis al-Jalis*, according to the Galland version, can be compared with the lyric verses of the Persian poet Khaqani, who died in 1200. The captain of the ship that brought the two lovers to Baghdad begins the passage.

" 'There is that great and marvelous city, where a general

and perpetual crowd of people can be seen from everywhere in the world. You will find an uncountable multitude there, and you will not have the unbearable cold of winter nor the excessive heat of summer; you will enjoy a springtime which lasts forever with its flowers, and with the delicious fruits of the autumn.' The two young people walked for a long time along the gardens which lined the Tigris, and they skirted one which was enclosed by a beautiful and long wall. Arriving at the end of it, they turned onto a long, well-paved street, where they saw the garden gate and a beautiful fountain near it. The gate, which was quite magnificent, had a decorative vestibule in which there was a sofa on each side. The garden belonged to the caliph, and in the center of it there was a pavilion that was called the Pavilion of the Paintings, because its main decoration consisted of paintings in the Persian style, done by several painters from Persia for whom the caliph had sent expressly. The large and superb salon formed by this pavilion was lighted by eighty windows with a chandelier in each one, and the eighty chandeliers were lighted only when the caliph came to spend the evening and when the weather was so calm that there was not a breath of air. They then gave off a very beautiful light that could be seen very far into the country on that side and into a great part of the city.

"Nur al-Din and his lady friend continued to walk and arrived at the Pavilion of Paintings which was in the center. They stopped to contemplate its admirable construction, its size, and its height, and, after they had gone around it, looking at it from all sides, they went up to the door of the salon on a large white marble staircase. There, in addition to the paintings, the sofas were magnificent."

Nasir's reign, the longest in the Abbasid caliphate, lasted almost forty-seven years. The relative calm of this half-century makes the caliph Nasir appear to be a great monarch. A capital thought of Claude Cahen seems to contain a great deal of truth: "The caliph Nasir probably had in mind a sort of universal Moslem pontificate over the sects." This may, in fact, be the case. In any event, the grave political events which followed, the Crusades and the Mongol invasions, make any conjecture useless. Doubtless, from the very beginning, there was the threat from Ghengis Khan's hordes to the east, but they were rather far off and did not constitute an immediate danger for Mesopotamia. To the west, after Saladin's victories had once again brought glory to the Moslem world, his successors maintained a certain amount of temporary equilibrium in Syria. Nasir is presented to us as a monarch who was very much aware of the current of public affairs. His political experience is praised, although we have no good proof of it.

The qualities that historians find in him seem to be quite commonplace. One of them says, "He was imposing, daring, well informed, and courageous; besides, he had good judgment, a ready reply, and an intelligence and insight which were always alert." In short, he ran the intricate machinery of government with understanding.

One detail makes us believe that he was the hero of *The Thousand and One Nights*, rather than his famous predecessor Harun al-Rashid, whom these tales have immortalized in the West. We are assured of the following: "Nasir, like his early predecessor, was in the habit of walking through the streets of Baghdad at night to keep up with the needs of the people and to be aware of criticism that could be formulated. Government employees and private citizens all feared him and remained distrustful, as if the caliph were observing them in their own homes. He sent many spies and informers among princes in foreign lands." An important comment for our hypothesis is, "There were extraordinary anecdotes about him in this matter." This is indeed the role attributed to Harun al-Rashid in the *Arabian Nights* tales.

For Yaqut, who died in 1299, Baghdad is still "the mother of the world, the mistress of countries," although in his detailed accounts he does not fail to point out ruins which are so prevalent that abandoned land and piles of rubble separate various districts from each other.

During the same period, Harawi furnishes information only on centers of pilgrimage. He knows the tombs of the Alid saints in the Quraish cemetery and the tombs of the Abbasid caliphs in the Rusafa cemetery on the west bank. That is where he locates Ibn Hanbal's sepulchre. A recent tradition at that time had transported this tomb from the Quraish cemetery to Rusafa. He indicates the location of Abu Hanifa's mausoleum in the neighboring cemetery, called Khaizuran.

The historian Ibn Kathir is triumphant when he speaks of the years 1192–93: "The caliph's army conquered territories from Raiy, Ispahan, Hamadan, from the whole of Khuzistan and from other regions. The caliph's authority was imposed, and this was the end of princes and principalities." Obviously, the long, rather calm reign of Nasir, at least in the capital, justified all these hopes.

It was during the time of this caliph that there was an organization incorrectly called "knighthood." Claude Cahen was the first to inform us about the movements of the urban masses, among whom he sees "the development of a certain municipal pride." He also proves his originality by trying to show the closeness of the *ayyar* and the *fityan*, which is related to *futuwwa*. He writes:

146

"A series of irrefutable pieces of evidence proves that there is sometimes synonymy and always association, in any case, between the two. In practical terms, the *fityan* appear as leaders and cadre of the *ayyar*. Upon reflection, one sees clearly what brings the two together. In both cases, they are outlaws in the true sense of the word. In both cases, vocation or necessity maintains behavior based on internal solidarity. There is more to it than that. We see, too, through several irrefutable pieces of evidence, that, among the *fityan* who are most aware of their moral aspirations, it is considered normal and commendable to steal, if it is done loyally in the interest of the group and only to the detriment of the rich. In brief, we find here, in an elementary way, a sort of class action. At certain moments, the action by a small group gives way to a desperate and heroic mass uprising."

In support, Cahen cites a concluding passage from the *Book of the Misers*, by Jahiz. Recently discovered texts seem also to prove him right. It is through these sources that we have come to know a *fityan* house in tenth-century Baghdad. We should not forget the ninth-century poem which gives the war cry of a member of these groups when he attacked, "This is for the *fata ayyar*!"

Claude Cahen continues: "It was normal that among the *fityan* certain minds should evolve toward the desire for consecration, for purification of the moral values implied in their earlier attitude. The success of the *fityan* attracted to them, in addition to those who were *ayyar* from birth, members of the middle class, indeed sometimes of the aristocracy, who were perhaps ambitious but also sincere and who, with their adherence to the *futuwwa*, did not lose their earlier religious culture or their decent temperament." The caliph Nasir "reforms the *futuwwa* in order to try to remove from it its anarchic and rebellious behavior, and he reinforces the characteristic which unifies the entire social ladder from top to bottom."

Arab authors place the supposed birth of the brotherhood called the *futuwwa* in the year 1207. All members of the upper bourgeoisie strove to join it, "from the most humble to the greatest." A large number of aristocrats put on the trousers of the *futuwwa* and received the special cup from which they were supposed to drink. We should not, in any case, see the *futuwwa* only as an "artisinal pact among Moslem workers," as Louis Massignon did in a burst of enthusiasm.

After having reorganized the pigeon range, the caliph Nasir intensified the pigeon-shoot competition. There was a great deal of talk about the betting that took place.

After the capture of Jerusalem, the sultan Saladin sent a certain number of Frankish prisoners to Baghdad in 1189. They were marched through the city to the sound of music, with their flags carried upside down, as was frequently the custom. He also sent the caliph the cross that the Christians had placed over the Dome of the Rock. It was buried under the Bab al-Nubi, one of the gates in the caliph's stronghold, and thus, the gilded copper cross was trampled on by all passers-by.

Although city disturbances were less frequent, they continued to bloody the streets of the capital. The fights kept on between the Shi'ites of Karkh and the Sunnites of the Basra Gate, one of them occurring in 1185. In 1205, a serious riot took place between the inhabitants of the two neighboring districts of Bab al-Asaj and Mamuniya in the southern part of the west bank, to the south of the royal palaces. Men fought with bows and arrows and knives. A great number of buildings were looted. In 1232, a violent fight broke out between the inhabitants of two districts. Participants fought with bows and arrows, slings, and bricks. Many people were wounded, and the troops were called out to separate the combatants. That the people were stirred up was evident in 1242 when violent fighting began between clans who intended only to have a good time.

In 1250, a military mutiny was brought on by withholding the troops' salary. Some historians accuse the vizier Alqami, who at best played a questionable role in the terrible events that were to cause the destruction of Baghdad and the fall of the Abbasid dynasty. He probably took this step to weaken the caliph, for his Shi'ite convictions made him an enemy of the ruling dynasty. Also in 1250, the government forbade the Shi'ite Muharram celebration in the Karkh district, for reasons of public safety.

In 1255, a violent fight took place between the Shi'ites of the Karkh district and the Sunnites of the Basra Gate. It was particularly bloody and occurred at the very moment when the Mongol danger should have been obvious to a large part of the population. Sent out to break up the fight, the troops erected barricades between the two neighborhoods. During the same year, the inhabitants of the Rusafa and the Abu Hanifa districts came to blows. The authorities had a difficult time calming things down, and many people were killed. It is in this final period of the regime that writers mention *ayyar* difficulties for the last time. The *ayyar* plucked turbans off the heads of passers-by and stole clothes in the bathhouses; they were also involved in a serious quarrel in the northern part of the city.

The people of Karkh continued their usual misdeeds, and it took nothing less than the caliph's intervention to restore relative peace. In 1257, an attack against Karkh by the Sunnites was significant because the properties of the vizier Alqami, a Shi'ite, were looted. This looting was probably the minister's motive for favoring Mongol plans.

At the beginning of the thirteenth century, people began to talk about the Mongols for the first time. Troop movements worried the public authorities. But even earlier, in 1217, the shah of Kharezm had arrived in Hamadan at the head of four hundred thousand men and made it clear that he intended to march on Baghdad. As he prepared for combat by distributing arms and subsidies, the caliph Nasir had his ambassador, Shihab al-din Suhrwardi, deliver a message to the shah of Kharezm. The envoy was treated with great scorn. He was asked to approach the shah's throne but was not permitted to sit down. Here is his account:

"Admitted to an audience, I arrived at a huge tent which had an entrance way such as I have never seen anywhere in the world. The hangings of this entrance were of satin, and the cords were of silk. In this vestibule were the princes of Persia, lined up according to their importance, the lords of Hamadan, Ispahan, and Raiy. We entered another tent made of silk and cotton. In its vestibule were gathered the lords of Khurasan, Merv, Nishapur, and Balkh. In the vestibule of a third tent the princes of the Transoxiana waited. Such were these three tents.

"I was then admitted to the presence of the Shah, who was staying in a tent with wooden poles covered with gold from which hung fringes mixed with precious stones. The monarch was a young, long-haired man, who was seated on a very simple throne; he was wearing a Bukharan tunic which must have been easily worth five thousand dirhams, and his head was covered by a piece of hide that was worth one dirham. I greeted him, but he did not return my greeting and did not ask me to be seated. I began to speak, and, in an eloquent discourse, I enumerated the qualities of the Ab-basids and I stressed, in the case of the reigning caliph, his ascetic and modest life, his piety and religious spirit. The interpreter translated my words. When I had finished, the interpreter said to me, 'Tell him. Does not the one you have just described live in Baghdad?' 'Yes,' I answered. 'Well,' he had the interpreter say, 'I am going to install a caliph who will be gifted with these qualities.' Then he dismissed me without giving me a letter of reply.

"A snow storm caused them to lose a great number of their pack animals. The shah of Khirezm's horse stumbled, and the sovereign considered this a bad omen. Indeed, things became confused in his army and there was a shortage of rations. He had brought with him seventy thousand Chinese. God made him turn back, and we were delivered from that frightful scourge."

This extraordinary ambassador was none other than the famous Sufi, Suhrawardi, whom the caliph Nasir held in particular esteem and for whom he built a monastery. Lodgings surrounded by a beautiful orchard and a bathhouse were installed for him and his family. He taught in Baghdad and died there in 1234. His tomb is an object of great veneration even today.

Then the beginning of the real Mongol threat to Baghdad appeared. Panic stricken, the caliph Nasir called for the help of the Ayyubids against Genghis Khan, but the Ayyubids were battling the Crusaders. It was a false alarm, and the successor to the caliph, Mustansir, convinced himself that the good old days were about to return, since he had been able to enlarge his territory by annexing Arbela in Upper Mesopotamia after the ruler of the city, Kökburi, died in 1233. Perhaps this was a safety measure, since it was learned the previous year that Mongol troops had penetrated

Azerbaijan and the suburbs of Shahrazur. The caliph mobilized his troops and asked other princes to co-operate in his defense efforts.

In 1236, pigeons were used to warn of the presence of Mongol contingents in Upper Mesopotamia heading toward Mosul. The caliph ordered the mobilization of the Bedouins of the area and sent out an army. It was another false alarm, just like the attempted siege of Arbela the year before.

The nature of these incidents, which were nothing more than looting raids, probably reassured the caliph's government. However, at the beginning of 1238, there was growing anxiety when messages announced new movements of the Mongol army which seemed to menace Baghdad. The caliph took no chances, and in the palace mosque he called for a holy war. The Moslem army set out immediately to meet the enemy. The first engagement was favorable to the Moslems, and the arrival in Baghdad of the heads of several Mongol warriors removed all apprehension. Although this was only a battle of the advance guard, the caliph's government thought it wise to have troops concentrated at the ramparts. In the meantime, the arrival of reinforcements sent by the Ayyubid princes of Baalbek and Damascus increased the number of the caliph's troops. The real battle took place on June 17, 1238, near Khaniqin, to the northwest of Baghdad, on the Khurasan road. It was a bloody rout for the caliph's army, and those who fled died of hunger and thirst. In Baghdad, there was great dismay.

The people became calm once again upon discovering that the enemy army was not advancing and that it had, in fact, returned to Persia. Both sides sent ambassadors. The Mesopotamian envoys were received in Qazvin, but we know nothing of the terms of the agreement which must have been reached. Fearing new attacks, the caliph ordered the ramparts to be repaired. Damaging Mongol raids in Upper Mesopotamia were still mentioned in 1244.

A certain amount of building construction gives evidence of the caliph's energy during the first part of the thirteenth century. Ibn Jubayr stated that a violent flood of the Tigris carried off a pontoon bridge. In the *Fakhiri*, we read that the historians, without too much accuracy, state that the caliph Zahir built "the bridge which still exists today" during his short reign of about one year.

It was during this period that monastery hospitals were established, as well as hospices where the poor were welcomed during Ramadan. Pilgrims who stayed in them received, upon departing, provisions for their trip, clothing, and one dinar. These hospices were known as Dar aldiyafa, "hospitality hotels." Writers say that this innovation began in the year 1205. Mutton and excellent bread were prepared in the hospices, and a considerable crowd of poor people was fed in them. The number of these buildings grew so large during the reign of Mustansir that there was one in each district of the city. We are told that the caliph was very generous and distributed alms to the needy, widows, and orphans.

Establishment of monasteries took place during the period of the Great Seljuks, but the monasteries prospered especially during the thirteenth century, perhaps under the influence of the Qadiriya brotherhood, which was organized after the death in 1160 of the famous mystic, Abd al-Qadir Jilani.

But we should stop at the famous Talisman Gate, which was also called the White Gate. It was closed from 1638 on so that no one could go through it after the Ottoman sultan, Murad IV, when he conquered the city. In 1917, the gate was destroyed as the result of an explosion. Fortunately, we have excellent reproductions of it showing brick walls with an opening which seems smaller than it really is because it is in the center of a solid tower.

This gate is worthy of our attention for two reasons. First, there was the sad and melancholy text which was written above it in 1221, after the time of the do-nothing caliphs who had lived under the yoke of the Buyids and the Seljuks and several years before the disappearance of the caliphate: "Here is what was ordered done by our lord and master, the imam of believers, al-Nasir li-din Allah, caliph of the Master of Worlds, God's total arguments over his creatures; may his call be a beacon of good direction on the plains of truth, may obedience to him be obligatory for believers, for their ears and for their eyes!"

Second, there was a surprising decoration over the arch of the gate, which is the reason for its being called the Talisman Gate. Van Berchem describes it thus: "In an admirable style, two dragons faced each other with their uncoiled tails decorating the spandrels of the arch of the gate and twisting into several knots; there was a tufted wing on their backs, and a sharp tongue extended from their gaping mouths, armed with fangs. These two giant and horrible beasts were separated by a haloed and richly dressed person, wearing a diadem, who held seized in his two hands the two menacing tongues. It was thought that this person represented the caliph crushing his two most feared enemies, the Shah of Kharezm and the Mongols."

If we consider only the aesthetic aspect, this piece of sculpture gives evidence of a highly developed artistic sense. The two dragons are imposing, despite the constraining demands of the curvilinear surface.

Another building, the Mustansiriya school, was still "the most beautiful monument in Baghdad" in the fourteenth century. It was in the south, near the Bridge of the Palaces. After having served as a hide-out for bands of brigands, it was used as a customs storehouse. More recently, the rulers of Iraq have tried to save it and to honor what remains of it by turning it into an archaeological museum. Henri Saladin says, "It is a rectangular structure, covered by vaults resting on a series of big, parallel arches; on the second floor a balcony is supported by cantilevers in the form of very elementary stalactites. From the inside abutments spring thin arches which are joined together by small vaults; the vaults are decorated monochrome mosaics."

The wall decoration, made of impressed brick, was very pleasant in the remains of the building. Louis Massignon described in detail the arrangement of these bricks. "It consists of reinforcing the joining of the bricks by diagonal, criss-crossed links, formed by bricks with small, square heads, marked with four-pointed stars. They are sunk into the wall like nails by increasing their length so that they are twice as long as the other bricks." The foundation inscriptions were very fine and stood out in relief on a background of delicate lace. What remains of the building confirms the judgment of Ibn Battuta and Mustaufi, who believed it to be the most beautiful monument in Baghdad. It is possible that the school, founded in 1227 by the caliph Mustansir, had great goals. According to its last historian, the large university contained four separate law schools for the four rites of the Sunnites, a house for the study of the Koran, another for teaching tradition, a library, a large room for mathematics courses and the science of succession, a building reserved for the teaching of medicine, pharmacy, and the natural sciences, with a hospital, and a kitchen, a bath, and storerooms for provisions. According to Ibn Battuta, "The teacher takes his place under a small wooden canopy, on a chair covered with rugs; he sits on this in a grave and quiet attitude, wearing robes of black and his black turban, and with two assistants on his right and left, who repeat everything that he dictates."

Other buildings deserve brief mention. In 1229, a monastery was opened which was founded by the caliph Mustansir near a mosque whose minaret foundation had just been laid. The same year, or perhaps a little earlier, the Qumriya mosque, supplied with rich furnishings, especially rugs and silver and gold lamps, was established on the east bank, on the edge of the Tigris. It was restored in the eighteenth and nineteenth centuries, but is interesting only because of its splendid brick minaret, which is circular and massive. In 1230, by order of the caliph Mustansir, the construction of the wall around Rusafa was finished. Also in 1230, the same caliph ordered the repair of the Karkh mosques, which had been damaged by the great flood of 1217. They had been secularized. Imams and muezzins were installed in the new sanctuaries. In the same year, a belvedere overlooking the Sarat Canal was built near the Basra Gate. In 1231, a school founded by the emir Iqbal Shirabi was finished in the al-Adjam *suq,* on the boulevard not far from the al-Sultan *suq.* The caliph Mustansir had the palace mosque repaired and enlarged. He ordered its restoration so that students from his school could attend theological discussions which were held there. In 1242, the caliph Musta'sim founded a library in his palace, and four years later his vizier, Ibn Alqami, did the same in his private residence.

Weather conditions in the middle of the thirteenth century were particularly bad. In 1217, there was a flood in Quraiya, which was on the edge of the west bank of the river, downstream from the pontoon bridge. Ibn Hanbal's tomb was seriously damaged. We will not say any more about this misfortune than we will about the fight between inhabitants of two neighboring districts which took place the same year near the Bab Azaj.

In 1224, torrential rains stopped all traffic for several days near the Basra Gate and in the Muhawwal district.

In 1248, incessant rains filled the sewers. The overflow of the Tigris was frightening. The west banks were submerged and the effect was especially disastrous in the Harbiya, Karkh, and Khuld districts. The people who lived along the river had to evacuate their homes and seek refuge wherever they could. Several mosques collapsed. The water reached the area surrounding the caliph's palaces, and many markets were destroyed. The Mustansiriya school was seriously damaged. Two months after the water receded, there was a new flood, worse than the previous one. The city's ramparts were damaged and several towers were cracked. Entire neighborhoods, such as Rusafa, were covered by water. Many buildings were swallowed up.

In 1255, a serious flood resulted from the overflow of both the Tigris and the Euphrates. Many neighborhoods were covered with water, and the mausoleum of Ma'ruf Karkhi was damaged. This catastrophe, which struck all of Lower Mesopotamia, did much damage in the city itself. There were serious economic consequences, such as the difficulty of getting supplies through and the raising of rents and prices in general. Many buildings were damaged, the most important of which were the mosques of Mahdi in Rusafa, of the palace, and of the sultan. The water reached the Nizamiya school. As is always the case under such circumstances, looting occurred in the city. The infamous *ayyar*, of course, took advantage of the windfall, and there were fights of a religious nature.

The year 1256 was marked by one of the worst floods in

the history of Baghdad, as far as duration and area covered are concerned. Water overflowed both banks, demolished a great number of buildings, and flooded all the east-bank markets. There was water everywhere; even the upper floors of houses were submerged. Wells overflowed and water backed up out of the sewers. The people sought refuge on the terraces. The caliph's palace was completely surrounded by water, and could be reached only by swimming or in a boat. The poor people screamed for help as volunteer rescuers carried children on their shoulders. The area within the walls around the caliph's stronghold was the most severely damaged. The Nizamiya school was almost completely covered. Dikes were hastily thrown up between districts. The rabble took advantage of the situation to loot, and frightful disorder soon followed, since most homes had been evacuated. Public prayers were held somehow in the Mustansiriya school, which could be reached only by boat. Most of the city was covered by the flood, which lasted about fifty days.

There is little to be said about the flourishing of literature. Historians continued to edit works contained in countless tomes. These works are valuable and we do not intend to treat them with scorn, but none of the writers give evidence of vigor or talent. They are honest memorialists who classified in chronological order the events that impressed them: highly important political events, anecdotes of lesser urgency, and the usual obituaries after accidents, fires, and floods. Ibn Jauzi, who died in 1200, was an exception. He was a Hanbalite preacher, who attracted crowds by his worth and his ardor, and a tireless polygrapher whose work records the life of Baghdad in that period.

The thirteenth century, however, was the most significant

period for the illustrated book. The "Baghdad School" was the most important of the names given to this flourishing art form. It was called, too, Arab painting, because the illustrations were made for works in the Arabic language and were painted in countries where Arabic was spoken. We have to be careful not to be deceived by this. Madame Sourdel-Thomine put it very well when she said, "We cannot fix with certainty the conditions under which this style was elaborated nor do we know what the stages of growth and development were." The same can be said of the paintings of the Baghdad School as of pre-Islamic poems. It was a perfect art, even if we know nothing about its faltering beginnings and cannot uncover the successive influences on it.

The painted manuscripts of the period concerned specific disciplines. There were treatises on botany, medicine, or pharmacy, works on automatons, collections of fables, and that very Arabic series of the *Seances* of Hariri, about which we shall say more.

The oldest, dated 1199, is the *Book of the Theriaca*, in the Bibliothèque Nationale in Paris. The most recent poses a problem. It is a copy of the *Encyclopedia* of the Faithful Friends, a work which is not very orthodox. Its date, which we know from its colophon, is 1287. It was illuminated in Baghdad. This work, which appeared thirty years after the Mongols destroyed the city, proves clearly that not all intellectual and artistic activity had ceased. Thanks to Richard Ettinghausen, we are familiar with two of its miniatures, and we can confirm that they "incarnate the purest Baghdad style at the height of its technique and when it was most irresistibly creative and dynamic."

It is a beautifully vigorous and powerfully original art,

with a great sense of proportion. The paintings are unparalleled because of the boldness, audacity, and mastery of the artists.

A manuscript of the *Fables of Bidpay* (in Arabic, *Fables of Kalila and Dimna*) is kept in the Bibliothèque Nationale in Paris. One scene shows two jackals killing a camel and is an excellent example of calligraphy. The two animals are tearing their victim apart with gusto while a crow does its best to attack one of the camel's eyes. Showing a satiric streak, the artist elsewhere presents a sultan-crow, duly crowned and planted firmly on his feet in the pose of an eaglet. He is sheltered by a bush which is slightly inclined, in imitation of a parasol, the symbol of sovereignty, and he stands on a rock instead of a platform. The crow's mouth is open as he gives advice to five cranes standing on the ground, which is covered with small flowers. The position of their necks and their staring eyes say a great deal about the state of stupefaction of this strange audience. This picture alone shows the major characteristic of the Baghdad School, a marvelous sense of fantasy and humor. In the strictly pictorial aspect, aside from the harmony of the colors, there is an uncomplicated and successful balance, good composition in which each figure has its own significance while blending in with the whole.

Manuscript No. 5847 of the Bibliothèque Nationale in Paris is justly famous. It has great merit aside from its many paintings (ninety-nine). The book, dated 1237, is a copy of Hariri's *Seances*. The illustrator was so pleased with his work that he signed it; his name is Yahya ibn Mahmud Wasiti. We know nothing about this remarkable artist except that he was of Aramaean ancestry, since one of his forebears was named Kawarriha. This painter was a good observer of the different aspects of everyday life. Through him, we are present at official processions, the departures of caravans, and even at incidents occurring during a voyage on the Indian Ocean. He shows us the arrival in a village, the interior of a library, and a sermon in a mosque. We even accompany Yahya Wasiti into a tavern.

The artist is a true master of composition and grouping. He does everything possible to develop both synthesis and detail. In a herd of grazing camels are two animals browsing on grass and eight other that are remarkable because of the curve of their necks, the position of their heads, and the color of their coats. Upon looking at the bottom of the picture, one has the impression that not a single foot is missing. In another picture, the hooves of the horses and mules give a massive impression, especially since the animals are carefully placed in rows, with their ears aligned, as they stand unperturbed by the noise of kettledrums and trumpets. The border is properly ceremonial since the picture portrays the official announcement of the end of the Ramadan fast. In the background are fluttering banners bearing the Islamic confession of faith and passages from the Koran. On the left is an immense standard, and on the right the painter uses long trumpets as though to mark a point beyond which the horses are not to go. There is a happy blend of freedom and obedience to the law of symmetry. The horsemen's faces are expressive. The standard-bearer is fully convinced of his mission, while his neighbors have the resigned look of military men used to taking orders. The musicians blow into their instruments as though enraptured, but the kettledrum player, leaning forward, seems to be afraid that he is not going to strike hard enough. All these details help depict the grandeur of the ceremony.

The departure of a caravan for Mecca is treated, on the other hand, with incomparable verve. We no longer see soldiers and guards' standards, but rather a popular orchestra and the oriflammes of the brotherhoods. The camels' lips appear to be trying to be graceful, and the position of their heads is portrayed with a certain amount of caustic humor. In unusual contrast, in the foreground is a placid horseman whose mount is no more bothered by the surrounding noise than is his master.

Let us examine one last scene which is remarkable because of the contrast in facial expressions portrayed in it. Thirteen individuals seem to be spellbound in the presence of the mocking hero of the *Seances*, who proposes a riddle to his listeners, with the secret hope, almost always fulfilled, of getting some money out of them. Each face deserves detailed study, as each expresses the curiosity and also the distrust of people attracted by the charlatan's pitch. But this is not the work of a brutal caricaturist. The irony here is more caustic than malevolent. The painter does not have a tormented soul; he has observed without hypocrisy the idle curiosity of the times and shows no desire to censure morals.

The qualities of realism, of observation of the world, of pictorial art, of careful and meticulous drawing make this copy of Hariri's *Seances* the uncontested masterpiece of Islamic painting.

These reflections coincide with those of the scholar who has best judged Arab painting, Richard Ettinghausen. He wrote: "It is to Baghdad and perhaps also to other cities in the south of Iraq that the greatest freedom and the strongest realism return. The figures are placed logically in their context, whether it consists of landscapes, sometimes treated with real concern for description, or architecture."

When his work is compared with these admirable paintings, the calligrapher Yaqut Musta'simi comes off second best in the opinion of Europeans. He spent his entire life in Baghdad, under the protection of the last caliph, and he died in the city at a very advanced age, in 1298. He was a remarkable, unspecialized artist, who put his most illustrious predecessors in the shade. His very personal habit of surrounding his lines of writing with sinuous clouds is characteristic.

We are now coming to the final tragedy. Beginning in 1243, Mongol detachments came within view of Baghdad from Arbela. The caliph ordered preparations to ward off any eventuality, but this was only a false alarm. Historians note that Mongol envoys arrived in Baghdad in 1246, which caused rather nervous commentaries. In 1252, the Mongols invaded and sacked Mesopotamia.

Finally, in 1257, there was a persistent rumor that the Mongol army, commanded by Hulagu, was approaching. But not even the verification of this rumor could bring the caliph Musta'sim out of his lethargy, awake any spark of energy in him, or induce him to take any action. The more talk there was of the Mongol sultan's plans, the more the caliph showed his lack of concern and his negligence. He no longer saw matters as they really were, and he did not realize how powerful were the forces against which he would have to defend himself. We are told that he took pleasure only in the company of buffoons and in listening to music.

His vizier knew very well what the situation was. He wrote him constantly to try to get him to ready the city for defense and to bring him out of his listlessness. He gave advice without stint to try to awaken him and press him into action, but the caliph became even more apathetic. The prince's courtiers persuaded him that there was no immediate danger and no need for alarm, and that the vizier was exaggerating the worrisome situation in order to increase his own importance and to raise taxes, presumably to ready the troops but really so that he could keep part of the money. Thus the caliph kept sinking into an even deeper sleep, while the enemy's activity kept increasing. Even in the face of this danger, battles still went on between Sunnites and Shi'ites. The caliph's vizier, whose role during this period comes under suspicion, backed the Shi'ites. Moreover, the attitude of the Shi'ites in the Karkh district was rather suspect.

A Mongol document leads us to believe that Hulagu, aware of the strength of his forces, which he perhaps wanted to use elsewhere, offered the caliph Mongol protection analagous to the Buyid and Seljuk symbiotic arrangement with the caliphate. We read in a letter written by the Mongol sultan: "The gate of Baghdad had never been closed (to the kings of Dailam and to the Seljuks) to any of the races who had established their domination there. How would entrance into the city be forbidden us who possess so much strength and power?" But it would be vain to try to rewrite history.

The Mongol sultan's army advanced as far as Hamadan, where it stayed some time. From there Hulagu sent envoys to Musta'sim. An ambassador was finally sent by the caliph, and, when Hulagu heard his statements, he realized that the court of Baghdad was just trying to gain time. Mongol troops were then sent on to Baghdad, and one detachment crossed the river and got to the west bank. When all the Mongol troops had arrived, one of the caliph's detachments came up to engage them in battle to the west of the capital. In the beginning, the caliph's soldiers seemed to be winning, but the sultan's army renewed its offensive, killed a great number of the enemy, and took many prisoners. Then an advance guard penetrated the western ramparts, and the soldiers spread out to loot the city.

On January 11, 1258, a cloud of dust appeared to the east and covered the city. People climbed to their roofs and to the top of the minarets to see what it was. They saw the sultan's army, his cavalry, his equipment, and those following the troops. The army surrounded Baghdad on all sides, and the siege machines began an infernal bombardment. The caliph's soldiers defended themselves and tried their best to push back the assailants, but on February 5, the Mongol sultan's banners appeared on the ramparts of Baghdad. The attack was mounted against the Bastion of the Persians, which formed the southeast angle of the ramparts. The fall of this tower brought about the rout of the caliph's army. The sultan's troops rushed en masse into the streets, killing and looting. The disaster which befell the city was terrible. Finally, the caliph, accompanied by his harem and his children, went to the sultan's headquarters. The caliph was strongly denounced for his nonchalance, his weakness, and his lack of concern. At last the curtain fell. The caliph Musta'sim was executed on February 10.

We have stressed the sovereign's indolent nature, but we should add that he did things, or let his vizier do them, which alienated the people. The vizier had stirred up the hatred which existed between Sunnites and Shi'ites. The troops were called in to restore order, and Karkh, the Shi'ite center, was attacked. The militia, completely out of hand, rushed in for a general massacre. The vizier's behavior in this incident indicates that he was playing some sort of double game. Many Arab historians accuse him of having been in league with Hulagu.

The imperialistic aims of the conquering Mongol soon became evident. The Moslem world was stunned to learn of both the conquest of Baghdad and the suppression of the Abbasid caliphate. February 10, 1258, marks the end of a type of regime whose survival was only fictitious: the caliph was no longer very important. However, a prediction had been made to Hulagu, who for a time was influenced by it, that if he killed the caliph, "the equilibrium of the world would be broken, the sun would be eclipsed, and there would no longer be any rain or plants." This shows that the Moslems attached a kind of legendary importance to the person of the caliph.

Before leaving this terrible catastrophe which struck the Moslem world, we should mention that Arab writers have stressed the atrocities committed by the Mongol troops. By order of Hulagu, a great effort was immediately made to clear away all traces left by the siege. Religious buildings and tombs venerated by the people were restored.

Of course, some of the damage was irreparable, but it was not as widespread as certain authors would have us think. The Mansur Mosque was spared, the Palace Mosque was restored, and four hundred manuscripts were saved from destruction in the Tigris through the efforts of Nasir al-din Tusi. According to certain Moslem sources, however, Tusi was the instigator of the caliph's execution. Tusi died in Baghdad in 1274 and was buried in the Shi'ite cemetery where Musa ibn Jafar's tomb is located.

Hulagu protected the Christians, probably at the request of his wife, who was a Nestorian. Although the fall of Baghdad itself was perhaps not vitally important, it constituted a terrible threat to the future of Islam. The following excerpt is from the text of a Christian historian of the time: "The city had been founded 515 years before. During all the time that it conserved the empire, like an insatiable leech it swallowed the entire world. Then it threw up everything it had taken." This quotation gives some explanation of certain anti-Christian and anti-Jewish explosions that occurred in

Baghdad during the second half of the thirteenth century. This type of demonstration against non-Moslems had not often been spoken of in the Mesopotamian city.

This was indeed the end of an age. The new empire that was born was not structured according to the old formulas. It developed in several kingdoms, Mongol, Ottoman, and Mamluk in Egypt, which divided all the territory of the caliphate.

From the commercial point of view, a new factor became important. From that time, the route from the Indies ended at Trebizond or at Tabriz.

Culture also felt the backlash of the disappearance of a world whose intellectual accomplishments were already diminishing. The libraries had been more or less the victims of the series of political or religious disturbances in the Abbasid capital. Although he was certainly rather frivolous, the last caliph, imitating some of his predecessors, gathered a collection of many manuscripts. It seems that all these books were thrown into the Tigris by order of the Mongol sultan. A historian later says, not without exaggeration, "The works of the colleges of Baghdad were swallowed up by the river, and their pile formed a bridge over which horsemen and foot-soldiers passed, and the water became completely black after having absorbed the ink of the manuscripts."

SURVIVAL

PEOPLE LIVING AT THE TIME OF THE SIEGE which crushed the inhabitants of Baghdad did not realize the great importance of what was taking place. There was, however, a new factor which was quite dangerous; the attacking army was not Moslem. After Hulagu's troops did away with the caliphate, Baghdad was no longer the political and cultural center of Islam. The Mamluks of Egypt, before giving refuge to a scion of the Abbasid caliphate, had tried first to restore a caliph in Baghdad. This attempt failed completely.

Our account stops with sad memories among the ruins of one of the metropolises of the Islamic world, one of the great cities of the universe. Almost all of Mansur's early Round City and the districts surrounding it on the two banks of the Tigris have disappeared, and even many of the place names have been changed. Almost nothing is left, or at least no building remains intact, of the ancient monuments erected by the fabulous princes of the Middle Ages. Houses have been built haphazardly on almost all the sites.

Louis Massignon writes that the old Round City "is now covered by a low, badly cultivated plain, full of ravines and deformed by floods, on the right bank between old Karkh to the east and the tombs of the two Shi'ite imams in Kazimain, to the northwest."

Before rapidly describing the political changes in the city, let us use Ibn Battuta's words as a preface. The information which he gives us may not have been entirely accurate in his time, since he uses Ibn Jubayr as a source. He begins his description with a lyrical couplet which almost leads one to believe that the fall of the caliphate was only a dream. "The City of Baghdad, the city of the Abode of Peace and capital of al-Islam, of illustrious rank and supreme pre-eminence, abode of the Caliphs and residence of scholars." The selection doubtless gives off a certain perfume, but it is the perfume of a bouquet of faded flowers.

We can now quote his observations which are not borrowed from his predecessor:

"The eastern part of Baghdad has magnificent bazaars and is splendidly laid out. The largest of its bazaars is one called the Tuesday bazaar, in which each craft occupies a section by itself.

"There are two bridges in Baghdad, made fast in the same manner as we have mentioned in describing the bridge of the city of al-Hilla, fastened upon a continuous row of boats ranged from bank to bank, the boats being held in place both fore and aft by iron chains attached on either bank to a huge wooden beam made fast ashore. The population are continually crossing them, night and day, men and women; indeed they find in this unending pleasure.

"Of mosques in Baghdad in which the khutba is pronounced and the Friday services are held there are eleven, eight of them on the west bank and three on the east bank. As for the other mosques, they are very numerous, and so too are the colleges, although these have fallen into ruin.

169

On the eastern side there are three mosques. One is the Caliph's mosque, which is adjacent to the palaces and residences of the Caliphs. It is a large cathedral mosque, containing fountains and many lavatories for ablutions and baths. The second cathedral mosque is the Sultan's mosque, which is situated outside of town, and in proximity to it are palaces designated as the Sultan's. The third cathedral mosque is that of al-Rusafa, which is about a mile from the Sultan's mosque.

"In the center of the Tuesday bazaar, is the wonderful Nizamiya College, the splendor of which is commemorated in a number of proverbial phrases, and at the end of it is the Muntansiriya College. All four schools are included in it, each school having a separate iwan, with its own mosque and lecture room. Inside this college there is a bath-house for the students and a chamber for the ablutions."

Our traveler lists a number of burial-places, first among which were those of the Abbasid caliphs in the Rusafa district. He locates in the same region Abu Hanifa's tomb, over which there was a large dome and a chapel where anyone who asked was fed. He adds that it was the only place at that time where food was doled out. The tomb of the imam Ahmad ibn Hanbal was also near by. It had no dome. This tomb was greatly venerated by the people of Baghdad, most of whom were followers of the imam's rite. Not far away were the tombs of Shibli, Saqati, Bishr Hafi, and Junaid. "The people of Baghdad have one day in each week for the visitation of one of these shaikhs, and the day following it for another shaikh, and so on until the end of the week.

"On the western side there are several sanctuaries: the tomb of Ma'ruf Karkhi, in the quarter of Bab Bassorah; the tomb of Musa ibn Dja'far, and beside it the tomb of Djawad; both of these tombs are inside sepulchral chambers and surmounted by a platform veneered with wood which is covered with plaques of silver.

"The Hospital lies between the quarter of Bab Bassorah and the quarter of al-Shari', on the Tigris; it is a vast edifice in ruins of which only the vestiges remain.

"The bath-houses in Baghdad are numerous; they are among the most sumptuous of baths, and the majority of them are painted and plastered with pitch, so that it appears to the spectator to be black marble. In each of these bath-houses there is a large number of cubicles, each one of them floored with pitch and having the lower half of its wall also coated with it, and the upper half coated with a gleaming white gypsum plaster; the two opposites are thus brought together in contrasting beauty. Inside each cubicle is a marble basin fitted with two pipes, one flowing with hot water and the other with cold water."

Beginning in 1258, Baghdad had become the capital of a province governed by a Mongol officer and housing a Mongol garrison. After the death of Ilkhan Abu Sa'id, it became the capital of a little state founded by Hasan Buzurg, the chief of the Mongol tribe of the Jalairs. He became an independent sovereign of Azerbaijan and Mesopotamia. This was the beginning of the Jalairid dynasty, in 1339.

The Great Black Plague of 1348 did not spare the city of Baghdad. We are told that anyone stricken became aware of it when a large abscess appeared on his face. He would die immediately after touching it with his hand. Sheikh Hasan was besieged in Baghdad at that time. Death suddenly raged through the army, which was trying to take the city, and forced it to lift the siege. Twelve hundred men, six generals, and a considerable number of pack animals died.

We mention the flood of 1356 because it was the subject

of a Persian manuscript painting which is now in the British Museum. A poet of that time says, "The large city was destroyed by water; the Devil take the river! Alas! Poor garden of Baghdad, paradise city, ruined by that wretch."

A little later the Mirjaniya was built as both a school and a mosque, a three-story structure around a central rectangular court with inscribed panels repeating the entire text of the terms of the *waqf* that was drawn up to support the establishment. It was founded in 1357 by a freedman of the Mongol dynasty, Mirjan. This mosque appears to be especially important because of its epigraphs and its state of preservation. It is the oldest monument of the medieval city, since what remains of the Mustansiya is in pitiful condition. It is also important because of the founder's desire for independence, which was never fulfilled.

In 1282, the new Ilkhan, Ahmad Takudar, announced to the people of Baghdad his conversion to Islam. There was no longer any question of re-establishing the Abbasid caliphate, which had taken refuge in Egypt. After the Mongol khans had become Moslem converts, the entire question of the fall of Baghdad became insignificant. It remains true, nonetheless, that the idea that the city was the capital and center of the caliphate was lost forever. This was the supreme humiliation and the real tragedy.

Another catastrophe struck the country. Tamerlane had taken Shiraz and had sent its sovereign's head to Baghdad where it was paraded through the streets. Then Baghdad was attacked and taken on September 4, 1393. According to an Arab historian, this was done to bring to his senses Ahmad ibn Uwais, who was detested by the inhabitants of the city. Ahmad fled without waiting for the arrival of his adversary. In the midst of violence and looting, the Mongol conqueror took time to repair Ibn Hanbal's tomb, which had been damaged by recent floods.

The prince of Baghdad took refuge at the Mamluk sultan's court in Egypt, then returned to his capital in 1394. This led Tamerlane to attack again. He camped outside the walls and laid siege to the city for almost forty days. He attacked the starving inhabitants in July, 1401, and mercilessly put them to the sword. This massacre and the material damage is summed up in a single sentence, full of black humor, by Jean Aubin, "Not a single representative of Timurid power remained; he would have served no purpose."

Ahmad did come back, however, to repossess his throne and to rebuild the city. But the Turkoman lord of the Black Sheep Family from Azerbaijan did not give him time to do so. He took over Baghdad in 1410, and, in turn, yielded to his rivals of the White Sheep dynasty in 1467. The historian Maqrizi shows his disillusionment in 1437 with the following words: "Baghdad is in ruins; there are no mosques, no faithful, no markets. Its canals are dry for the most part, and it is difficult to call it a city."

In 1508, the new Safavids of Persia took control of Baghdad. The Safavid shah at that time was sovereign of a large kingdom that stretched from Baghdad to Armenia and from the basin of the Upper Euphrates to Khurasan.

Twenty-five years later the Ottoman sultan, Soleiman, conquered Baghdad, solemnly entering the city in 1534. The stages of Soleiman's expedition are found recorded in a Turkish manuscript now in the University of Istanbul. Among its miniatures is a view of Baghdad which is of even greater interest because the manuscript is dated 1537. The Safavids recognized the Ottoman sultan's sovereignty over Baghdad in the Treaty of Amasya (1535).

Then there was a short fifteen-year period of Safavid occupation, which seems to have been disastrous for what remained of the city's monuments. But the Ottoman empire did not remain inactive. Sultan Murad IV began his campaign in 1638 and took Baghdad, which he entered ceremoniously. The Ottomans became masters of Baghdad, and they set a pasha over the little provincial capital. The occupation of the city seemed almost to have a magic air about it. The Talisman Gate, through which the Sultan entered, was walled up for all time. He visited the sanctuaries and the tombs of Abu Hanifa and Umar Suhrawardi and Abd al-Qadir Jilani's mausoleum, which had just been repaired.

In the middle of the seventeenth century, Baghdad must still have looked rather impressive from the outside, with its crenelated walls and numerous towers surrounded by a wide moat. Inside the northwest corner was a fortress. The thirty-four governors of Baghdad up to the beginning of the eighteenth century should not be blamed. They did make an effort to construct religious and public buildings in the city.

The entire eighteenth century marked an administrative period unlike any other in Baghdad's history. The Ottoman pashas were replaced by the Mamluks, and there were long years of relative security with very little to upset the daily lives of the people. In 1753, and once again ten years later, the sovereign of Persia, Nadir Shah, tried in vain to take the city by siege. Toward the end of the eighteenth century, Baghdad had to fight off attacks by the Wahhabi and two assaults by Fath-Ali Shah.

Baghdad underwent long, bloody sieges from the fourteenth to the twentieth centuries. The city suffered from frequent trouble caused by mutinies of the army that was supposed to defend it as much as from the looting raids of

174

the Bedouins who lived in the surrounding area. There were many recurrent, catastrophic floods as well as epidemics.

It was to ward off the danger of the floods that the governor Midhat Pasha, who was to become a famous statesman before his miserable end, had the city's ramparts removed and a solid dike erected. The effort was only partially successful.

The name appears again in connection with the famous Baghdad Railway. At the end of World War I, the British army took Baghdad on March 11, 1917. The Lausanne Treaty set up the Kingdom of Iraq under British mandate. Baghdad became its capital. King Faisal took the throne in 1930. A republic was proclaimed in Baghdad on July 14, 1958, as the result of a military coup d'état.

11.

CONCLUSION

CLEMENT HUART'S JUDGMENT of the people of Baghdad should be added to Ibn Jubayr's and Mustaufi's, which were quoted earlier: "In the midst of mishaps and catastrophes, the inhabitants of Baghdad, with justifiable pride, never forgot that their city had been the capital of the great Abbasid empire; they were never able to resign themselves to the secondary role that fortune seemed to reserve for them; their haughty spirit did not readily admit that their city had become a provincial town. This is what explains the agitated and undisciplined character of which they gave evidence time and again. We know today of numerous riots and uprisings, some of them victorious, others cruelly suppressed. Baghdad never remained peaceful for any length of time, and that is what makes its history interesting."

Very great names in world political history, with their glorious and victorious retinues, come to mind when we study Baghdad. Founded by the Abbasid caliph Mansur, it becomes, in *The Thousand and One Nights*, the focal point of the adventures of another caliph, Harun al-Rashid, who was so popular in the West. The Buyids and the Seljuks left their mark, a well-earned one, even if their celebrity proved short-lived. Baghdad was ravaged by Hulagu's and Tamerlane's hordes. And finally, the Ottoman sovereign, Soleiman the Magnificent, entered the city with pomp and ceremony, after having unseated the Persian Safavids.

Topographic information remains somewhat doubtful, despite the zeal and various techniques of Guy Le Strange and Louis Massignon. The present little book should not be counted upon to give the precise details. I believe that it does give sufficient information on the activity in the different sections of the city. I have not, however, been willing to give any figures on Baghdad's population, since the estimates encountered here and there during my reading have seemed fanciful and exaggerated.

Except for a very brief résumé, I have not gone beyond the conquest of Baghdad by the Mongols in 1258. My object was to paint a picture of a civilization which had as its center and guiding light the city of Baghdad, the metropolis of the Abbasid caliphate. From the cruel Mongol conquest to this day, the little provincial city has been deprived of its former renown. I hope, with the people of Baghdad who are justly proud of their past, that there will be a rebirth of the city's ancient glory.

HISTORICAL TABLE

Caliphs

Mansur	754–775	Radi	934–940
Mahdi	775–785	Muttaqi	940–944
Hadi	785–786	Mustakfi	944–946
Harun al-Rashid	786–809	Muti'	946–973
Amin	809–813	Ta'i	973–991
Mamun	813–833	Qadir	991–1031
Mu'tasim	833–842	Qa'im	1031–1075
Wathiq	842–847	Muqtadi	1075–1094
Mutawakkil	847–861	Mustazhir	1094–1118
Muntasir	861–862	Mustarshid	1118–1135
Musta'in	862–866	Rashid	1135–1136
Mu'tazz	866–868	Muqtafi	1136–1160
Muhtadi	868–869	Mustandjid	1160–1170
Mu'tamid	869–892	Mustadi	1170–1180
Mu'tadid	892–902	Nasir	1180–1225
Muktafi	902–908	Zahir	1225–1226
Muqtadir	908–932	Mustansir	1226–1242
Qahir	932–934	Musta'sim	1242–1258

Buyids   945–1055
Seljuks   1055–1092

SELECTED BIBLIOGRAPHY

Annuaire du monde musulman. Paris, 1954. Pp. 187–96.

Auble, Emile. *Bagdad*. Paris, 1917.

Bagdad, numéro spécial d'*Arabica*, Vol. IX, No. 3, pp. 229–485. Leiden, 1962.

Benjamin of Tudela, in Adler, Elkan Nathan. *Jewish Travellers*. London, 1930. Pp. 43–48.

Canard, Marius. *Histoire de la Dynastie des Hamdanides de Jazira et de Syrie*. Algiers, 1951. Pp. 155–74.

Coke, Richard. *Baghdad the City of Peace*. London, 1927. (With an extensive bibliography, pp. 330–32.)

Duri, A. A. *Baghdad*. In *Encyclopedie de l'Islam*, 2nd edition.

Huart, Clement. *Histoire de Baghdad dams les Temps modernes*. Paris, 1901.

Ibn Battuta. trans. Sir Hamilton Gibb, The Hakluyt Society, Second Series, no. CXVII. Cambridge, 1962.

Ibn Jubayr. trans. R. J. C. Broadhurst. London, 1952.

Lassner, Jacob. *The Topography of Baghdad in the Early Middle Ages*. Detroit, 1970.

Le Strange, Guy. *Baghdad during the Abbassid Caliphate*. Oxford, 1900.

Makdisi, George. *Autograph Diary of an Eleventh-Century*

Historian of Baghdad, Bulletin of the School of Oriental and African Studies. XVIII–XIX. London, 1956–1957.

———. *Ibn Aqil et la resurgence de l'islam traditionnel au XIe siecle.* Damascus, 1963.

———. *The Topography of Eleventh Century of Baghdad, Arabica.* VI. p. 178–197, 281–309.

Massignon, Louis. *Bagdad et sa topographie au moyen âge: deus ources nouvelles, Opera minora.* Ill. Pp. 88–95. Beirut, 1963.

———. *Les medresehs de Bagdad, Bulletin de l'Institut Français d'archéologie orientale.* VII. Pp. 77–86. Cairo, 1909.

———. *Les saints musulmans enterrés à Bagdad, Opera minora.* Ill. p. 96–101. Beirut, 1963.

———. *Mission en Mésopotamie, Mémoires de l'Institut français d'archéologie orientale.* Cairo, 1912.

Miskawaihi. *The Experiences of the Nations.* Ed. and trans. H. F. Amedroz and D. S. Margoliouth. Oxford, 1921.

Nicholson, Reynold. *Literary History of the Arabs.* London, 1907.

Rousseau, J. B. "*Description du Pachalik de Baghdad.* Paris, 1809.

Salmon, Georges. *L'Introduction topographique à l'Histoire de Bagdad.* Paris, 1904.

Sarre, Friedrich, and Herzfeld, Ernst. *Archäologische Reise in Euphratund Tigris-Gebiet.* Berlin, 1900.

———. *The Lands of the Eastern Caliphate. Cambridge,* 1905.

Streck, M. *Die alte Landschaft Babylonien.* Cambridge, 1900.

———. *Baghdad.* In *Encyclopedie de l'Islam.* 1st Edition.

Ya'qubi. *Les Pays.* Trans. Gaston Wiet. Cairo, 1937.

INDEX